Mya meets Elin or Love meets Light

ALSO BY KATE ROUSE

The Diary of a Happy Dropout

Still a Happy Dropout

A Spiritual Handbook for the Modern Era

A little bit of Poetry

Mya meets Elin
or
Love meets Light

Kate Rouse

ZEPHYR
Publications

MYA MEETS ELIN OR LOVE MEETS LIGHT

Copyright © KATE ROUSE 2020

First published by Zephyr Publications, Queensland, Australia, 2020

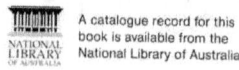 A catalogue record for this book is available from the National Library of Australia

Author: Rouse, Kate

Title: Mya meets Elin or Love meets Light

ISBN: 978-0-6487165-2-5 (pbk)

Subjects: Religious and Spiritual fiction. Self-help and Personal Development. Mind, Body, Spirit.

All Rights Reserved

No part of this book may be reproduced in any form, by photocopying or by any electronic or mechanical means, including information storage or retrieval systems, without permission from both the copyright owner and publisher of this book.

This book is a work of fiction.
The author asserts her moral rights.

Desktop Publishing—Wendy Blake 2020
Cover Design—Wendy Blake 2020

For my beautiful nieces, Stephanie, Ella, Phoebe and Eliza,

May their lives be full of adventure, clarity and contentment

And for all young people, everywhere, seeking meaning and purpose in this often complicated and challenging era

Acknowledgements

A huge thank you to my life partner, Shayne, for believing in me, supporting my dreams, and having incredible patience. Thank you to our property, Bahwyn Horse Stud, for giving me the space, peace and freedom, to allow words to flow. Thank you to our horses, for keeping me grounded and dreaming. My aunt, Gill Herbert, provided kind assistance, for which I am ever-grateful. Another aunt, Sal Huxtable, has been enthusiastic and supportive, which I appreciate greatly. My lovely, farmer friend, Gordon Gannon, provided positive encouragement, which helped propel me forward with editing. My ever-supportive friend, Mardi McCarthy, after reading the manuscript, was full of fervor, and her strong belief in what I am doing, reinforced my chosen pathway, as challenging and obstacle-filled as it is. A special thank you, yet again, to Wendy Blake, for her desktop publishing assistance and designing the beautiful cover. Finally, I would like to thank my beautiful mother, Alice Rouse, who has always been there for me and supported my goals, despite me not following conventional paths.

About the author

The eldest of four sisters, Kate Rouse grew up in Albury and on a small farm at Table Top, New South Wales, Australia. She had a happy childhood with freedom to explore nature and enjoy life with horses, that were a huge part of her life then, as they still are today.

After completing a BA and Dip Ed at the University of New England, Armidale, Kate worked at Mt Hotham and Mt Buffalo in various roles and travelled extensively throughout the world for 12 years, interspersed with teaching English in Japan and casual teaching in New South Wales and Victoria. She self-published two travelogues in the 1990's.

During the following 12 years, Kate worked as a teacher, Aboriginal Education Worker, youth worker, pool manager, factory hand and receptionist. She travelled in Australia with her partner, Shayne, completed Certificate IV in Community Welfare, a Diploma of Counselling and a Fine Arts Certificate.

At Christmas, 2010, Kate was struck down with pneumonia and during this time she contemplated her mortality. Slowly recuperating, while house-sitting in Queensland, Kate began to think about what she would write in a book if her life was coming to its finality, when the idea of, "A Spiritual Handbook for the Modern Era," emerged in 2012. Kate wanted to help others who were experiencing trouble or confusion and provide some clarity with relevance to the sometimes complicated and often demanding era we find ourselves in today. Kate published the book with Zeus Publications in 2013. She re-published in 2019 under her own publishing company name—Zephyr Publications.

During another bout of illness, in 2014, Kate wrote, "Mya meets Elin or Love meets Light," sitting beside a fire while the cold, southern winter blustered outside the frigid mansion (still house-sitting). Kate wanted to write a novel which shared the ideas in, "A Spiritual Handbook for the Modern Era," and make them more readable and memorable for teenagers, aged 14 and up. A few edits later, the manuscript was printed out as a booklet, shared with a few people and gifted to her nieces at Christmas. It remained in a bottom drawer until 2019. This time, it was having no power one week, due to a broken-down inverter, that brought out the manuscript for pencil editing. Many edits later, it was ready for publication. Kate had put out a call for help on Facebook, and fortunately for her, her old school friend, Wendy Blake, put up her hand. Wendy assisted Kate greatly with her desktop publishing and cover design skills in 2019, and again in 2020.

Kate and Shayne now live in Queensland where they are establishing a small horse stud. Living with Chronic Fatigue and its many challenges, Kate writes and paints when she has the energy to do so. She has experienced life broadly, felt life deeply and studied spirituality from an early age. Kate and Shayne share their lives with Teuco, a talkative, blue parrot, Whispit and Sox, mischievous, tabby cats, and 12 beautiful horses.

Contents

1. Mya 3
2. Troubles 7
3. Walks 19
4. Elin 21
5. Soothing Words 25
6. Insight 31
7. Words of Wisdom 39
8. Difficult Decisions 47
9. Nature 57
10. Mya's Future 63
11. Challenges 73
12. A Solution 83
13. For Young Adults 89
14. Middle and Later Life 107
15. The World as it is 113
16. New Horizon 119
17. The Spiritual Life 123
18. Last Days 137
19. Holidays 141
20. Change 155
21. Looking Forward 165

Chapter One

MYA

My name is Mya. Mya means love in Nepalese. My parents were hippies and they were on their round-the-world tour after university when I came into being. They say I was their love child, made in Nepal, hence my name, Mya.

I love mountains—the clear air, the majestic views, blue valleys below. I love horse riding and walking there. I'm always asking Mum and Dad to take me to the mountains. "Oh, that's just because you were made in the mountains," they joke. Actually, on the Annapurna Circuit, a true mountain baby. I hope to go there one day. It's one of my dreams.

My parents aren't hippies anymore. They have a furniture building business in a regional town and we live in a rustic, old, white, weatherboard house on a small farm nearby. Inside are polished floor boards, colourful rugs, and interesting artifacts Mum and Dad collected overseas. Patchwork quilts, made by an old family friend, add to the atmosphere. It's a very cosy home. We have Murray Grey cattle, Damara sheep and horses. I love horses—all animals really—but horses especially. We have a golden New Zealand Huntaway named Sefton. We bought him to round up the sheep, which he does well, but he is also one of my best friends. I love him dearly.

I'll give you a brief description of myself. I know when I read books, I like to imagine the person in my mind's eye. I'm 14 years old. I have long, straight, light brown hair, green eyes which people say remind them of the colour of cat's eyes, an average sized, narrow and slightly pointy nose and a little dimple on my chin. I wear my hair in a pony-tail most of the time. I go to a small private school, but I'm much happier at home—riding the horses, walking around the hills, helping Mum and Dad with farm work. I live in jeans and checked shirts.

I have a younger brother, Ben. He's 12 and looks like a typical Aussie beach kid with scruffy, blonde hair, blue eyes and freckles. We get on well, some of the time. He loves teasing me and that can be annoying. Ben chases me with yabbies he has just caught out of the dam, their claws menacingly grasping, or a dead mouse out of the traps. I run and scream. Everyone thinks it's hilarious—not me though. He just doesn't know when to stop—that can be a problem.

Mum looks like an older version of me and Dad looks like an older version of Ben. I think they like that, having a little Joan and a little Tom.

We have four horses. Goldie is a part-Arabian mare who shimmers in the summer with dark dapples gleaming. Her son is a grey, mostly Arabian gelding named Calypso. He is very friendly. I have trained him since he was a small foal. Zora is my black Welsh Cob—a gentle and reliable boy. Ben has a lazy, white pony named Casper. The horses are pivotal in my life.

I've been having a bit of trouble at school lately and it's affecting my whole life. I'm a sensitive and quiet girl who loves writing, art and nature. I can be hurt easily. Mum and Dad say I'm too sensitive.

Chapter Two

TROUBLES

I've been at this school for just over two years. I'm in Year 9 and we're about half way through first term. It's a strict place with lots of rules.

My best friend, Zoe, left at the end of last year. We were inseparable for two years. Her family has moved to another town. Zoe and I lived in our own little bubble—not really concerned about anyone else at school. Horses bonded us, as did the fact we were somewhere between the really academic, quiet kids and the popular, sporty, social girls. There are only 12 girls in our year—it's a small school. Zoe and I would sit under a large, shady oak tree for lunch overlooking a lovely, green oval lined by poplar trees. No one else went there. We'd talk about our horses and plans for the weekend, and boys a bit. Sometimes we'd play handball with the boys.

When Zoe told me in December that she was leaving, I was devastated. We enjoyed our last weeks together. Now she has gone and her departure has left a big hole in my life. She used to come home and ride all over the countryside with me. Sometimes I'd stay with her in town and we'd ride there. I miss her so much.

I was dreading coming back to school after the summer break without Zoe—not sure how I would fit in without her. I tried to fit in with the academic girls. That didn't really feel right. I played handball with the boys. Sometimes I went and sat under our oak tree—feeling sad and lonely. Other days, I immersed myself in books in the library.

There are five girls in the popular, sporty group. They must have observed my loneliness, as one day, about two weeks into term, they all approached me and the ring-leader asked if I would like to join their group. I was surprised, but readily agreed, "Yes, thank you."

As well as being popular, sporty, attractive and reasonably academic, they all acted as if they were 16 and tended to get into a bit of trouble. I'm shy, and found it hard to open up to them. One day they went shop-lifting—stealing lollies. I stole a few too—to fit in, but it definitely didn't feel right. Another day, while the year 11 boys were doing an English test at recess, we walked up and down the corridor passing the classroom—two of the girls had crushes on boys in that class. After about five trips past the windows, the English teacher walked out, his cheeks burning and bald head gleaming. The boys were laughing. "What do you girls think you're doing?" screamed the teacher.

"Just walking," replied the ring-leader.

"Well, you're disrupting my class. This is ridiculous behaviour. Come back here at the second lunch bell."

I felt mortified—so not me.

At lunchtime we were instructed to write 200 lines saying, "I will not parade in front of classrooms at any time. I will not cause disruption."

The group also wanted me to smoke. They smoke in the toilets and it smells terrible. "Come on, Mya. You'll love it," they urged. It makes me feel sick—just the smell of cigarettes. I refused, and that was a tick against me.

We always had lunch in the grandstand. The year 11 boys played cricket below it. I think that's why we were there. I like a boy in my Maths class. We sit beside each other sometimes, but that's all. I'm not interested in older boys and haven't had a boyfriend yet.

My shyness and lack of confidence made it hard to open up and be relaxed with these girls. I just followed them around and was quiet most of the time. They talked about boys, smoking, clothes, weekends, bands, sports and other kids. I really didn't have much in common with them, but I was trying to fit in.

One day, just after eating lunch in the grandstand, the girl who I like the most came over to where I was sitting. The others followed. She said, "Mya, we've decided we don't want you to be in our group anymore."

Tears welled up in my eyes and my face reddened. "Oh, poor Mya," said one, and it did seem sincere.

"That's okay," I responded, trying to put on a brave face. I picked up my lunchbox and walked as fast as I could to the locker room with tears pouring down my cheeks. I didn't feel at home amongst them, but harsh rejection is hard for anyone to handle—especially a lonely 14-year-old girl.

I fumbled with my bag, putting my lunchbox away, and then sat in one of the toilets, feeling miserable. "Oh, I hate it here," I thought to myself. "What am I going to do now?"

Fortunately, I had art class that afternoon. None of those girls are in that class. I immersed myself in a painting I was doing of Goldie.

Waiting for the bus was painful. I didn't look at anyone—just the clock—wanting that half hour to pass in a flash.

I felt numb as I stared out the window of the bus. Felt like I didn't care about what happened to me from now on.

At home, I did my daily chores and made sure Ben was okay, giving him his daily dose of chocolate biscuits and ice cream with homemade chocolate sauce. We're addicted to chocolate. Mum buys these huge boxes of chocolate biscuits we can free-range on.

After that, I walked out into the horse paddock and sat down, my head hanging, sobs emerging. "I hate myself. I hate my life at school. What's the point of anything?" I asked. "I'm too shy and too sensitive. Why does life have to be so hard?" The horses slowly walked over, and one by one, they nuzzled up to me, pushing my head, and then they all just stood quietly in a circle surrounding me, seemingly offering some empathy. I wouldn't normally sit in the paddock like that and their reaction was unusual, as normally there would be some squabbling amongst them. I reached up and gave them little pats. "Thank goodness for you."

Sitting at the dinner table that evening Mum noticed I wasn't my usual self. I told my family of the day's events. They were surprised—how could someone treat their Mya like that. I started crying. Mum walked over to my chair and gave me a hug. "You'll be okay, Mya. Be strong."

"I can't be. I hate that school, and I have no friends," I gushed, through tears and sobs. "It's hopeless."

"Oh, my poor darling. Don't go to school tomorrow. I'll take the day off and we'll do something special. I might even take you to the mountains."

"Thanks Mum."

That night I cried myself to sleep—feeling lonely, misunderstood, rejected. Is my life worth living? I hate myself.

The next day, as promised, Mum drove me up to one of my favourite mountains where there are horses available for trail riding. We went out for a ride amidst the snow daisies, granite boulders and snow gums. It is beautiful there, and the air is so fresh.

That did lift my spirits somewhat. I'm not sure I'm suited to school—maybe I should do home-schooling. Mum said we'll consider all options.

Fortunately, it was the weekend, so two more days away from that school and those girls. If I tried to forget about it and just concentrated on things at home, I didn't feel too bad, but when I thought about it, I was a mess—sad, lonely, rejected. I cried at night.

Mum and Dad said they'd like me to try and finish the term. They had already paid the fees and they thought it was a great school. It is good from the point of view of making you do your schoolwork and homework, as otherwise there are detentions and lines to do. I play netball and tennis. One of the English teachers is in my tennis team. Culturally, it is also good—I'm in the choir and we do plays—musicals and dramas. I have guitar lessons. All those things are positive, but when you're 14, the most important thing is friendship.

Decided to endure it. Didn't feel like I had much choice. Went back on Monday. Said hello to those girls, but that's all. Reverted to my oak tree, the library and handball with the boys. I'm sure the teachers were noticing, but no one said anything.

Felt numb—just carried out what I needed to do in robot fashion. Normally, I do well with my projects and tests, but I lost enthusiasm for doing any work. I got the lowest mark in a history test. The conservative, male teacher made a big deal of it in front of everyone. I wished the ground would open up and suck me into it. Tears formed. "Poor Mya," said my favourite of the five. Tried to keep a brave face—brave, red face. I was relegated to the lower history class, but I was actually glad, as the teacher was a sweet, old woman who was very gentle.

The days turned into weeks, and it all seemed too much to bear. I had one special friend, a year 11 girl. Grace has lovely, long, chestnut hair and large, brown eyes. She is very pretty, very mature and very kind. Every day she would check up on me. I'd tell her I'm okay. It's alright. One day, about a week ago, she gave me a letter with a poem. I read both slowly.

Here is the letter, "Dear Mya, Here is a poem which I'm sure will help you. I know you don't have it easy at school, mainly, I think, because you are years ahead of your classmates in kindness, sensitivity and other qualities which come from understanding.

"I won't say, 'best of luck,' for your future, but I will say, 'Make your life work for you,' and don't worry about what others say and think (that's very important—I've only realised that recently).

"Whenever you feel the need to talk to me, feel very free to do so. You're a good little person.

love Grace."

The poem—***We Must be Strong*** by Walter Rinder.

It is not enough that God gives us the gifts of love, gifts of physical beauty, gifts of talent; for those are only a few of the pillars which are rested in the foundation of our personality. The strength of this foundation is life. The building starts at birth. Its strength over the years, our mending the cracks, replacing the parts that crumble or are weakened by time; depend on our precipitation, our confidence, our giving and receiving, our interacting with life, our sensitivity, fulfilling our commitments and honouring our word. Also, the strength of this foundation depends on our understanding and overcoming hurts and pains, conditionings and fears. For these are the storms which can destroy (lay these pillars to ruin) or weaken our mind and body.

From birth until death these storms are constantly tearing down people who can't build the strength to stand against their might. Cities are full of these people and cities are the eyes of these storms.

So many human beings lie in the rubble of their own personalities.

Tears formed in my eyes as I read. Grace is so sweet and caring. Not many Year 11 girls would even think of a Year 9 girl. "Thank you, Grace. That is so thoughtful. I will cherish these for the rest of my life."

"You're a good girl, Mya. Don't worry about those other girls. They've got a long way to go to catch up with you."

"Thank you," I replied shyly. "It's hard though."

"I know," said Grace, hugging me. The end of lunch bell rang and we had to head back to the locker room. I wished Grace was my age.

That day, I had a library class in the afternoon. One of the academic girls invited me over to look at something on the computer. "Look Mya, someone has posted a horrible picture of you." I looked over her shoulder and saw the picture, an altered version of my school photo. I had horrible, straw-like hair, a monobrow, glasses, a moustache and beard. Underneath was the caption, "Dork of the Year." The picture had 10 likes.

My heart fell into my stomach. Tears welled up, yet again. "Yes, that's horrible," I mumbled, rushing out to the locker room.

"I'm useless. Ugh. I feel so sad." Despite Grace's words, I felt totally diminished.

Someone must have said something to the old history teacher, as she arrived soon and reassured me, "Everything will be alright, Mya. Don't worry about those girls." The meanest girl had created the post. So harsh.

I had another day off and when I went back to school, I was even more hermit-like—not good for a 14-year-old girl.

After attending to Ben's chocolate needs each day after school, I collect the eggs, move the sheep with Sefton if necessary, feed him and Whispit—oh, I forgot to mention him. He's a tabby Oriental cat (similar to a Siamese), full of mischief and he has that whiney meow. He follows me everywhere and has so much courage. He'll jump on the horse's backs and walk under them. I'm not sure if that's stupidity or courage. He is pigeon-toed and has a funny crisscross walk.

Our chooks are also unusual. They are Golden Spangled Hamburgs, a rare endangered breed. They are golden with black spots, and with their red crowns and white cheeks, they look quite flashy. I love watching them dust bathe and look for insects.

After my chores, I go for a walk or horse ride in the forest nearby. Ben usually goes off yabbying or ferreting with Craig, our 12-year-old neighbor. They are buddies. I spend a lot of time by myself, maybe too much.

When I was in Infants School some mean girls used to chant, "Mya, Mya, your pants are on fire." That was hard, but this is even worse.

So, that sums up my troubles.

Chapter Three

WALKS

Below our farm, there's a reserve, which leads into a forest. I can walk for miles there. Sefton usually follows me, and sometimes, Whispit comes too.

There's a beautiful stream with gurgling, white water bouncing over grey and white granite boulders. Mossy rocks line the banks. Ferns in crevices. Wattle trees and majestic mountain ash. A red and green flash through the trees—a beautiful king parrot. Currawong cries reach skyward. Lizards rustle in the undergrowth. Red robins, willy wagtails and blue wrens flit here and there. Occasionally I hear thumping through the bush, twigs breaking with every thump—a grey kangaroo or rock wallaby. Red and blue crimson rosellas add a splash of colour, vividly contrasting to the verdant surroundings. Sometimes, I am lucky enough to spy a lyrebird—standing on a rock or log—and in full song, warbling his own cries or mimicking Kookaburras, Currawongs, Magpies, Rosellas, or even chainsaws. They are amazing mimics. I love this little valley, and especially the area near the stream. There are blackberries and blueberries growing in some parts. Sometimes I eat a few.

I have a favourite, large boulder beside a secluded bend in the stream where the water slows down a little. I like to just go and sit there and enjoy the life-filled atmosphere—listening to the sounds of nature.

Sefton doesn't like sitting for long and usually goes off exploring.

Lately, most days, I've been walking—trying to walk out my pain. Some days, I just feel numb, but still go anyway. Other days, I reach my rock and sit there for ages, questioning my predicament. Everything seems so pointless. I hate this school, have no friends. I'm so lonely. Sometimes I question the point of life, my life, and wonder is living really worth it.

Chapter Four

ELIN

I'm walking along the stream's edge, with Sefton at my heels. I'm breathing in the damp, energy-filled air. I reach my rock and decide to sit for a while. As usual, Sefton goes off exploring and it's not long before I hear him barking. "Sefton," I call. "Sefton, come on boy." He doesn't respond, continuing to bark.

I go to investigate. Nearby, there's a large thicket of blueberries where a lovely woman is picking and placing berries in a golden, woven basket. Sefton is adding his noisy enthusiasm. I approach this luminous woman. "Sefton, come here boy." He heeds my call this time and runs over to me. "Sorry about that," I shyly apologise for Sefton's antics. "He gets a bit carried away sometimes."

"No no, that is no problem," replies the woman, as she approaches me and gives Sefton a pat. He is settling down now. She has a strange accent, reminding me of a Swedish girl I met once. Her voice is gentle and almost seems otherworldly, with a melodic cadence.

The woman looks to be about 25. She has long, blonde hair, large, blue eyes and olive skin. She wears a knee length, white, cotton dress, pulled in at the waist. She is radiant.

"What's his name?" she asks.

"Sefton," I reply.

"That's a lovely name. What breed is he? I haven't seen a dog like that before."

"He's a New Zealand Huntaway. They're not so common in Australia. Huntaway is a funny name, as he's not a hunter, but a sheep dog. Maybe they named them that because they hunted the sheep. I'm not sure. I should google that."

"Interesting," replies the woman.

"Do you come here often?" I ask her.

"I've just started coming here lately. I'm new to the area, and when I discovered these berries, I decided to come and collect them. I like using them in my cooking and eating them fresh too. They are full of goodness."

"I know," I reply. "They're delicious."

"What's your name beautiful girl?" asks the woman who looks like a heavenly angel to me.

"Mya."

"Oh, love," she responds.

"Yes, not many people know that," I reply, surprised by her knowledge. "I was made in Nepal, so my parents named me Mya."

She chuckles, if you can imagine a harp-strung chuckle. "I am Elin."

"I haven't heard of that name before, but it's beautiful."

"It is an old name from my native land. It means light."

"It really suits you. It's a lovely name."

"Thank you, Mya. You are too sweet."

There is a thumping through the bush nearby. Sefton runs off in hot pursuit. "Oh, I better go and get this dog under control. I hope I see you again, Elin."

"You will, dear Mya." She smiles and waves as I walk off to retrieve the adventurous canine.

I walk home, almost in a trance. Was she real? Did that really happen? She seemed too unknown, too perfect. I can't believe that such an angelic woman could live in this harsh world. I don't tell anyone of my special meeting. I will just see how things progress.

Chapter Five

SOOTHING WORDS

I've had a bad day today. After the incident in the library, the girl who posted the picture has had to face repercussions. She is not a happy girl. All of the girls in that group are treating me coldly, but she is the worst. Today at the start of lunch, she approached me. "Mya, can't you just keep things to yourself? I can't go on the computers now because of you and my parents have banned me from social media. You're just a trouble maker. You don't belong here."

"I'm sorry," I mumble, my face reddening as tears moisten my eyes. "Be strong, Mya," I think to myself, but it's not working.

"From now on, just mind your own business," says the mean girl aggressively.

"Okay, I will." Off to the locker room again.

In my art class I lose myself in painting.

I'm now walking with Sefton down to my favourite rock adjacent to the stream. I sit on the boulder beside gurgling water under mountain ash and wattle trees, resting my head on my knees. "Everything seems so pointless, Sefton. School is just too hard. I don't fit in. I wish Zoe was still here." Tears. At least they release some of the anguish.

It's not long before I hear a melodic voice singing a beautiful song which almost sounds like nature herself. Elin is on the path nearby and spies me on the rock. She is in a blue dress today. She almost glides down to me. "Hello, Mya." She observes my tears. "Oh dear, what is wrong?"

"I've had a bad day today," I sob, as I climb down from the rock to stand beside Elin. "It's a long story."

"You can share it with me if you wish to do so," offers Elin.

I tell her of Zoe leaving, my not really fitting in with the girls at school, my isolation, the invitation to join the group and the smoking, shop-lifting and getting into trouble, the subsequent request to leave the group, the post and now what happened today.

"Oh Mya, that's so difficult," says Elin, giving me a reassuring hug. "Do you want to come and pick blueberries with me?"

"Okay," I readily agree.

At the thicket, Elin begins to pick berries and place them in her basket. "Bullying is a growing and terribly destructive problem," she says.

"I know."

"Empathy is the ability of a person to identify herself mentally with another and then understand the other's thoughts or feelings with compassion. With greater empathy, bullying could be diminished. People need to think of the results of their words or actions and imagine themselves in the place of others."

"I think that's hard for many young people," I observe.

"True, but it's something that needs to be discussed and children and teenagers can learn about these things at home and at school. They need to imagine themselves in the place of others."

"It's too easy for people to bully with mobile phones and the internet," I reflect. "I don't think that mean girl has it in her to develop empathy."

"Maybe, but you could be surprised. The bully's ego is causing destructive behaviour."

"Ego?" I query.

"That's the part of the mind that reacts to reality and has a sense of individuality."

"I see," I respond, placing a handful of blueberries in Elin's basket.

"It's true, that bullies lack empathy, but there is potential to change. Mya, you have been a victim of bullying. Remember, you are loved, special and important, a shining star. If you find yourself in this predicament again, remove yourself from the situation and seek help from friends, teachers, parents or school counsellors. Don't suffer alone."

"I've been doing a bit of that."

"If it happens through the internet or mobile phone, let others know, as action needs to be taken immediately. Don't let the bully destroy you. You are the strong one. Seek help, surround yourself in love, and light will overcome this darkness."

"Thank you, Elin. I'll try to keep that in mind, but it's so hard."

"I know, Mya. You also said you experienced peer pressure."

"That's right," I affirm, as I pick some hard to reach, juicy berries.

"Sometimes others may pressure you to do things you don't want to do, such as smoking. Stand your ground. If they continue to coerce you, you would be better off finding new friends."

"That's the problem. I don't think I can find new friends at that school."

"You will come up with a solution, Mya. I'll be here to help you. What do your parents think?"

"They want me to finish the term, but then they are open to me changing schools, or maybe doing home-schooling."

"Home-schooling could be a bit isolated for you," reflects Elin. "You learn by just being amongst other people. Everyone is different and people have so much to offer one another. Difference enriches life whether it be through ethnicity, cultural aspects, sexual preferences, religion, personal preferences of any kind, or creativity bringing forth your spirit to the world. You may be criticised and teased for your individuality, but do not let this hurt you—you are loved by God as you are and you are free to express your individuality in the modern western world. Those who tease or bully lack empathy, true confidence and awareness of themselves as spiritual beings. I think you are aware of that, Mya."

"Yes, I am. I've always believed in God and I talk to him often. Mum and Dad gave me a children's bible when I was five. I demanded it. I used to watch my grandfather read the Bible and that inspired me. Sometimes I go to a local youth group."

"You would have friends there," says Elin, now just focusing on our conversation.

"Yes, but they don't go to my school," I pause, then continue, "I understand what you mean about individuality enriching life. There's a gay boy in my year. He's a great actor and is very funny. He makes everyone feel happy."

"Well, that's one positive thing, and I'm sure there are many more. Can you think of any?"

"Yes, I love writing and painting. I have a good family and the best animals in the world." I pat Sefton to add impetus to my response.

"Very good. I'm sure we can find many more positive aspects to your life and soon things will get much better for you, Mya."

"I hope so," I reply, with a tone of pessimism in my voice.

"It's getting late. I better be getting home," says Elin, picking up her basket and covering the berries with a blue and white checked cloth. "I can meet you here tomorrow if you have time."

"Okay, thank you Elin. I'm very glad I met you."

"I'm equally glad, beautiful girl." She gives me a quick squeeze. We say goodbye and walk off in opposite directions. I am not quite so sad now, feel better able to cope.

Chapter Six

INSIGHT

I flop onto my bed after another bad day at the end of cold glares. "It's all so hopeless. I feel useless. I hate myself. I hate my life. What's the point of anything?" A black mood envelops me. I feel numb.

It's approaching the time that Elin will be at the berry patch. I force myself to trudge down the path. She's there already picking, wearing her white dress today. Elin greets me with a radiant smile, "Hello, Mya."

"Hello, Elin," I respond, with half a smile.

"Did you have another bad day?" asks the wise woman, sensing my sadness.

"Yes, just bad vibes and looks. I'm feeling really flat, hopeless. It's like I'm in a black hole."

Elin stops picking and looks at me directly. "Oh dear, that's a challenging feeling, and it is very common. Many people experience it at some time in their lives."

"I didn't know that," I reply.

"Yes, it's true. The black emotion of depression may leave you feeling isolated, misunderstood and hopeless. It's important to seek help from a doctor, counsellors, friends and family. Don't let it destroy you. There is a light at the end of the darkest tunnel. In your darkest moment you will not agree with that, but really, truly, there is. Don't give up. God is there for you. He will listen too."

"That's reassuring," I reflect. "I'm really glad I met you, Elin."

"Me too. You haven't had suicidal thoughts have you, Mya?"

"Some days, but I don't think I could actually go through with it," I reveal my darkest thoughts.

Elin looks very concerned. "If you have suicidal thoughts of any kind, seek help immediately. Things may be terrible, but PLEASE remember the gift that is your life and there is something to live for—your family, friends, pets, your passions."

"Yes, I've been trying to think about that. My family, horses, Sefton, Whispit, my art, writing. I care a lot about all of those things."

"Mm, and that's what connects you to life—gives you a reason for living," reassures Elin, as she leans against a large granite boulder.

"I know," I reply, as I sit on a smaller boulder beside her.

"If you feel depression is taking over your life, exercise helps, as does having little goals. Try not to be hard on yourself. Being in nature can also be of benefit and trying to do what you love, though you probably don't feel you love it anymore. However, as you undertake your previously loved pursuit, some inkling of satisfaction and sunniness may begin to re-emerge. Volunteering may also aid recovery. There is light at the end of that dark tunnel—I promise you. If you are on the spiritual path, spiritual work is healing. Nowness helps greatly."

"Nowness?" I query.

"That's one of my made-up terms. It means being totally present-centred, so you are totally present to those you are in communication with which makes them feel attended to. Being present-centred to the work you are doing, whatever you are doing, enhances your soul's journey as you are focused on the now. Mindfulness is the commonly used term to describe what I'm talking about.

"Nowness can be attained through creativity—being absorbed in painting, writing, baking or a myriad of other activities. It can also be attained through sport, such as skiing down a mountain, catching a football, snorkelling on a reef or through meditation techniques or communing in nature. Carry that nowness into everyday life and the results can only be positive. When you are washing the dishes or hanging out the washing, remember that nowness."

"That makes sense," I observe. "They sound like very useful ideas. I've heard of meditation, but I don't know anything about it."

"It's a way to centre in on the part of you that is spiritual and to relax the mind—to be free of the babble of the mind and rest in the infinite stillness. It can be achieved through peaceful relaxation in nature, gentle exercise, nowness, meditation classes or listening to guided meditation.

"Your whole life can be a meditative experience as you keep in mind that you are a spiritual being here to learn and give with awareness of your thoughts and feelings and your impact upon other human beings, animals, plants and the Earth. Conscious moment-to-moment living with awareness is soulful."

"I see. I think I understand. When I sit on the rock beside the stream I just tune into the water and feel like I'm almost becoming part of it and all of nature. I stop thinking and feel more like an observer."

"Good girl," commends Elin. "That's exactly it."

I haven't ever talked to anyone like this before on such a deep and wise level. Elin is adding a new and enriching dimension to my life. She is so angel-like.

"Thank you," I respond. "I think my depression will just melt away now that I've met you. I feel like I have some hope again."

"Yes, hope is very important. In most difficult situations there is hope for change or at least changing an attitude to the scenario. Life is about change. It cannot be otherwise. Challenging situations may seem impossible to deal with at times, but they are great opportunities for growth and progress—mentally, emotionally and spiritually. With greater awareness and clarity, you can move forward with optimism.

"Acceptance is important in life in general. Things will not always be as you desire. If you are not happy in a situation, try to accept it. Take steps to change and have patience. Life consists of ups and downs, and to keep on an even keel, useful tools are acceptance, gratitude and patience."

"I'll try to remember that."

"Getting back to coping with depression, it is good to focus on the little things," suggests Elin. "Try not to become enslaved by the past or concerned for the future. You will get better with little steps. You are loved by God and He wants you to heal as you learn to love yourself,

Him and all of his world. Having awareness of your negative emotions, how they affect you and those around you, and then healing that part of you is soulful work and part of a soulful life. Overcoming your fear, anger or any other negative emotion, will lead to greater harmony and peace on all levels."

"Wow, Elin, that's a lot to think about, but it all makes sense. How do you know all these things?"

"Oh, it's a combination of life experience, spiritual reading and practise and observation of people and nature."

"It would take a lifetime to learn all that, if not more," I acknowledge.

"Yes, I'm an old woman."

"You only look to be about 25 to me."

"No, I'm much older than that."

I feel it's impolite to ask Elin her age, so leave it at that.

Dusk is approaching. The twilight adds a lovely glow to the forest and pink streaks across the sky. "Thank you, Elin. I'm learning so much and you're making me feel more optimistic which I didn't think was possible."

"Anything is possible. As you work towards your dreams, and as long as it feels right, you will be amazed at times how life seems to be magical and flow effortlessly. You are living as you should and your energy is working well for you. The right people, opportunities and places will arise as needed and your light will shine."

"Such beautiful words," I reflect.

"You are a beautiful, sweet and sensitive girl, Mya. Believe in yourself. I do."

"Thank you, Elin," I reply, blushing. "I'll try.... I better go or it will be dark."

"Will I see you tomorrow?" asks my new friend.

"Yes, I'll be here," I respond. "I'll look forward to it."

Chapter Seven

WORDS OF WISDOM

It's Saturday and Mum and Dad have gone to a clearing sale. Ben and I go sometimes, but we find it to be a bit of a drag, traipsing around looking at machinery and old furniture. We like the scones with jam and cream though.

Craig's away at the moment and Ben's going through a phase of playing games on the computer which frustrates me as I'd rather he come for a ride. Today he totally refuses to—absorbed in a lengthy game.

I ride Goldie, weaving through the sun dappled forest on my golden dappled mare. The scent of eucalyptus is strong after a rain shower last night. Everything is fresh and refreshing. I haven't been riding much lately, and when I do, I'm just doing it, not really enjoying the ride, but today I appreciate it more. I think that's thanks to Elin, as I'm now feeling a bit better and looking at things slightly differently.

After my ride, Ben is still glued to the computer. "Mum and Dad won't be happy," I tell him.

"I don't care," he retorts.

"Why don't you go outside and go yabbying or something?"

"Don't want to while Craig's not here."

"Will you come for a ride tomorrow?"

"Don't know," Ben grunts, annoyed by my urging, his eyes glued to the computer screen where two men are having a sword fight.

"I give up." Exasperated, I wave my arms in the air and leave Ben to his preferred pass-time.

On my afternoon walk with Sefton I discover Elin at my rock. "I've been waiting for you," she says.

"Thank you," I reply. "I wouldn't miss this for the world."

"I'm not picking berries today. I have enough at the moment. Would you like to just sit here?" asks Elin, as she pats Sefton.

"Okay," I respond. After the rain, the stream is alive with water bouncing over rocks. Droplets bejewel feathery fern fronds. Everything seems more brilliant than usual—verdant and glowing.

I sit near Elin on another rock. "How has your day been?" she inquires.

"Well, I had a good ride on Goldie. I haven't been enjoying my rides lately. That's if I manage to go. It's been hard to muster the energy."

"I'm glad you enjoyed it. It can be really hard when you're depressed to do anything, and it's common to lose enthusiasm and optimism. Your feelings about your horse rides show you are starting to heal."

"Thanks to you," I acknowledge.

"More so to you. I'm just here to illuminate your path a little."

"Well, I appreciate you taking the time to help me and teach me."

"It's my pleasure beautiful girl. Now, did anything else happen today?"

"I'm having a bit of trouble with my brother, Ben. At the moment he just wants to sit on the computer playing games all the time. I try to get him to go outside and do something else but he refuses. He has a pony named Casper, who really needs some work because he's overweight. Lots of kids spend huge amounts of time playing video and computer games. It doesn't interest me."

"Hmm, that can be a problem," responds Elin. "Activity of a physical nature is important for the body, mind and soul. Children should not become chained to technology—the internet, television, video games, mobile phones. They are tools, not real life. Children need to explore and play outside. They need to have fun doing so and God will be smiling."

"I agree. At least when our neighbour, Craig, gets back, things should get back to normal. We have ice cream and chocolate sauce and chocolate biscuits after school and then Ben usually goes to play with Craig. He needs to burn off some energy at the moment."

"Oh Mya, that's an unhealthy afternoon tea. Everyone needs to eat a healthy diet of vegetables, fruit, grains, meat, fish, nuts, seeds, dairy and healthy fats. Sugar, fast food and unhealthy snacks should be minimised. Regular exercise through play, dance or sports is important. Keeping the body healthy through good nutrition and exercise will lead to greater energy and a clearer mind. This is all positive for body, mind and soul."

"That seems sensible, but I don't think I can get Ben to buy it."

"Hopefully he will change as he grows older. Mya, you said you love painting and writing?"

'Yes, amongst other things," I reply.

"It is important to find your talents and foster them but within realistic limits so that you enjoy them—that it does not become a painful struggle and destroy the outflow of your gift's bounty," explains Elin.

"One girl I know is being really pushed by her parents to be a tennis star, but I'm not sure that she loves tennis that much. She doesn't seem very happy, even though she is winning lots of games."

"Hmm. Parents need to foster their child's talents but within her desires, otherwise great potential may be harmed. It is their child's journey, not theirs, but parents pave the way providing opportunities for talents to flourish."

"My parents are pretty laid back—that part of the hippy still in them. Ben and I have a lot of freedom."

"Yes, it can be a difficult balancing act," adds Elin. "Through your art and writing, Mya, you are being creative which connects you to God. You can also be creative through play, sport, cooking, exploring, experimenting, building, music, dance, drama and gardening. Creativity leads to great peace and happiness."

"Well, I know when I'm painting or writing I really have to concentrate and I am in the moment—that nowness you were talking about Elin."

"Yes, that's right, and like I said yesterday, it is a form of meditation. I'm glad you have those interests, Mya, as that means you can always do that wherever you are and it will help you live a soulful life."

"Soulful?" I ask, somewhat perplexed.

"I use that to describe the spiritual aspect which reflects deep thinking and feeling. As you are creating, you are connecting to God and living soulfully."

"I think I understand. It sounds very positive anyway. I'm sorry, but I have to go home to do my chores Elin. I better get going."

"Oh, I'm glad you have responsibilities. As children grow older it is beneficial for them to have responsibilities around the home as this will prepare them for adult life. The responsibility of caring for a pet is also of value as they learn to look after another creature, develop love for it and hopefully all animals. When a child loses a pet, this is a good learning ground for the future experience of grief and loss in whatever form it may take. The connection with pets will hopefully foster a love for all of God's creatures and their habitats."

"I love my pets and nature but get a bit tired of my chores. Mum's trying to get Ben to do a bit, but he's on the lazy side when it comes to jobs. Sometimes he doesn't seem to respect Mum."

"That's another thing. Children need to learn to respect their siblings, parents, friends, elders, teachers and other people in general. With greater respect there will be greater harmony at home, at school, in society and in the world."

"Needed right now I think," I observe. "A lot of kids don't show much respect to adults. It's a problem."

"I know," agrees Elin. "Maybe I'll see you tomorrow, Mya?"

"You will." I give Elin a quick hug. She beams a big smile. I almost skip back home through the forest—that dark mood is lifting.

Chapter Eight

DIFFICULT DECISIONS

I am feeling much better—not so pessimistic, not so depressed, not so misunderstood. It would be different if I hadn't met Elin—she is a light, so true to her name, in my current darkness.

Today Mum and Dad take Ben and I to our local pub for lunch. My brother and I always have fish and chips—not healthy but yummy. While we're waiting for our meals Mum says, "You seem much better, Mya. I've noticed that, especially in the last couple of days."

"Yes, I am. It's only a few more weeks until the end of term and I'm not worrying as much about those girls now."

"That's very good. Have you thought about what you want to do?"

"Well, I was pretty keen on home-schooling, but maybe that's too isolated."

"We think so," responds Mum.

Dad nods in agreement. "There's that school nearby where you can do equine studies," he suggests, "or you could go to the local high school."

"I'm not sure. I'm not so keen on going to another small, private school, but the high school seems huge and impersonal."

"You'll have time to think it over," says Mum. "We'll take you to both of them soon, and that will help you decide."

"Thanks Mum. It will."

I enjoy just being with my family—enjoy light-hearted conversation.

Elin is sitting on my rock. Sefton bounds up to her, his tail eagerly wagging. "Hello, boy," says Elin, patting him on the neck. "Hello, Mya. How are you today beautiful girl?"

"I'm fine, thank you. I'm feeling much better, thanks to you."

"That's great news."

A little brown bird flutters around our heads seeking insects, totally ambivalent to our presence. Elin laughs her musical chuckle. "I have some challenging ideas for you today, Mya. Are you up for it?"

"Hmm, I guess so," I respond, somewhat reluctantly, as I resume my place on the smaller rock.

"Just ideas to help you through life and to help you assist others," explains Elin.

"Okay, I'm ready," I acquiesce.

"Have you ever experienced child abuse or neglect?"

"Not neglect but sexual abuse only a few months ago unfortunately. It was horrible. There was an old man painting at our house and it was a student-free day. Ben was at Craig's place and I offered to help the painter. While I was painting, he undid the sides of his overalls and started pushing against me. It was disgusting. I manoeuvred away from him and walked into the dining-room. He followed me and then tried to hug me and kiss me. I turned my head, so he could only kiss my cheek. He held my arms firmly and asked me if I liked him. I said I didn't know. Whispit was distressed and I said I had to put the cat out. I went out into the paddock and caught Goldie and rode her around the hills for hours until Mum and Dad got home. He watched me from the verandah. It was creepy. I met my parents at the gate and told them what had happened. I was crying and it was hard to get it out. They were shocked and angry. At the house, Dad asked the painter to leave immediately and told him not to return. Mum and Dad decided not to take any legal action as they didn't want me to go through that trauma at such a young age. I just try to put it out of my mind, but I have a real distrust of old men now and I hate his name."

"That's not surprising," reflects Elin. "I'm so sorry you had to experience that, Mya. It must have been terrible." She climbs down from the rock and gives me a comforting hug.

"It was terrible. I've never had a boyfriend and that was my first physical contact with a male in that way."

"It may be worthwhile to see a counsellor to talk out the issues to help you heal. It would also be wise for your parents to report that man's behaviour to the police."

"They won't do that. As a family we have put it behind us."

"I see," Elin pauses, and then says, "Child abuse may be mental, emotional, physical, sexual or neglect. Children need to be made aware of what is unacceptable, abnormal behaviour from adults and other children and to tell a trusted adult if it occurs, so appropriate action can be taken without delay. They need to be encouraged to seek help despite threats from the abuser."

"Hmm, I've seen on TV that the abuser is most often a family member, friend or trusted adult in a supervisory role," I tell Elin.

"That's true," she agrees, "so it's important for children to be aware of these things, so action can be taken if it does happen."

I nod in accordance.

Elin returns to my rock. "Have you been having personal development classes at school yet?" asks this wise woman.

"Yes, it's very embarrassing. The teacher has been showing us pictures of male and female reproductive organs and explaining sex. The boys think it's a great joke and laugh a lot. The teacher gets pretty annoyed with them."

"Has he covered contraception yet?"

"No," I reply. "What's that?"

"It's tools to use to prevent pregnancy during sexual intercourse."

"Oh," I respond, surprised by the direction of our conversation.

My face obviously reveals my discomfort. "Don't worry, Mya. I just thought I'd cover a few things like this today. Would you rather I didn't continue?"

"No, no. It's alright. Go on," I encourage Elin.

"Well, it's important to learn about the available methods and be prepared with the method that suits an individual and his or her lifestyle. People may think they don't need such things but at times the unplanned event may happen."

"I haven't even had a boyfriend yet. That is the last thing on my mind at the moment. I know some girls do those things early, but I think Dad would kill me if I even kissed a boy."

"That might be good contraception then," laughs Elin. "But on a serious note, it is good to know these things early. Unplanned pregnancy can be a big shock and a very emotional time. If this occurs, it is important to ensure a girl (or couple) seeks help from a sympathetic doctor, a family member if possible, friends or counsellors—anyone she (they) can confide in. She (they) needs to take time to make decisions and needs a peaceful place to let clarity through. She needs to think about the outcomes of her decision and how it will make her feel in one year or ten-years- time. A girl in this situation should not be hard on herself, and remember that God loves her and will do so whatever choice she makes."

"That would be a very hard position to be in," I observe. "I'm not sure what I would do."

"That's why I'm telling you these things now," says Elin, "to help pave your way in life with insight and clarity."

"I appreciate that so much," I thank this shining light in my life. "I don't think anyone else would ever talk to me like this. I think every girl needs an Elin."

"That can be you, Mya. I'm passing on these thoughts to you, and then I hope you may pass them on to others."

"Well, I'm writing them in my diary," I respond. "Maybe I will publish it one day."

"I hope so," reflects Elin. "Now, where was I? Oh yes, I was going to talk about adoption next. There are many great potential parents out there eager to adopt, but that has to be a soul-felt decision as it can leave a parent broken and the child may feel rootless and confused when he discovers he was adopted. There are many ways to bridge the gap and it may be the best solution for everyone involved. Girls or couples need to think carefully, think slowly and think soulfully.

"For some girls, pregnancy termination may be their choice at this difficult time. If that feels right for them, they need to seek medical assistance. If not, they need to be careful not to be pressured by those around them as the result may be a heavy emotional scar, difficult to heal, and grief, difficult to resolve. If a girl requires a termination, it is advisable to seek counselling and her doctor can help organise things, or there is information in the phone book and on the internet.

"Immediately post-termination, it is preferable that a girl be in a safe and loving place where she can nurture herself as her body and soul adjusts to the changes she has just experienced. She needs to take time, try to be peaceful and release any emotions as they arise. She needs to be gentle with herself. If a girl experiences difficult emotions post-termination, counselling may be helpful. She could attend a Rachel's Vineyard Retreat[1] and speak with a spiritual worker. These things can help, but it can be a slow, hard road to tread, and in the end, there has to be forgiveness. God forgives and a girl needs to forgive those involved, and greatest of all, herself. She needs to love herself and let God's light and love through to break the clouds of darkness shrouding her heart, so it may sing songs of love to her soul, God and the world.

"At this time, rituals may help as they may in other areas of life. A girl can use flowers, rocks, ornaments, religious icons, letters, fire, water, soil, whatever feels right. She can speak, sing, dance, paint, write her thoughts and feelings, and ritual may help cleanse, release and bring her back into wholeness. While broken, girls are unable to progress wholeheartedly in their physical or spiritual life."

"That's a lot to take in, Elin. An unplanned pregnancy would be so difficult. It would be such a confusing time, and I imagine emotionally overwhelming."

"That's true for many girls, so I think it's good to talk about it as a potential thing that may happen—this may help with prevention or for

---

[1] www.rachelsvineyard.org.au

a girl to be better able to cope if it does occur. Everyone makes mistakes, but this is one of the more difficult ones."

"Yes, I imagine that to be so," I agree. "I hope I don't have to go through that, but who knows what will happen in the future?"

"It remains to be seen, Mya, but let's hope your road is paved with insight and clarity."

"That's happening right now," I observe.

Light is fading. The red sun is just sinking over the horizon and streaks of pink and purple fill the sky. "Time for you to go beautiful girl."

"Thank you, Elin. You're the best." A quick squeeze and goodbye.

"Wow, that was a lot to take in," I think to myself, as I wind along the path through the mountain ash beside the stream while Sefton scampers in the undergrowth.

I go to bed feeling less worried, more content and thankful for my new life lessons. Thank you, God. Goodnight.

Chapter Nine

NATURE

"Hello, Mya," Elin greets me, as she picks blueberries.

"Hi, Elin."

"I want to make a blueberry pie tomorrow, so I decided to stock up on some fresh berries."

"I'll help," I offer, picking a small handful.

"Thank you. How are you feeling?" asks my lovely mentor in her white dress today.

"Better, less worried and more content."

"That's good," affirms Elin.

"Your ideas were pretty heavy going yesterday," I continue, "but I wrote about them last night—wanted to write it down while it was fresh in my mind."

"Excellent. Today I want to talk about a lighter subject, but it is still of grave importance," says Elin, as she reaches for some ripe berries.

"Hmm," I nod, relieved today's topic will be somewhat less intense.

"You love nature, don't you?" states Elin.

"Yes, it's where I feel happiest," I respond, "and it gives me comfort, especially this place."

"It's the same for me," reflects Elin. "Nature gives me solace, peace and inspiration. It is positive if a love for nature can be fostered in children from a young age. If possible, it may be beneficial for children to experience wilderness, to learn to respect and love nature and carry that feeling into adult life to lead a harmonious existence on this troubled planet. In an untouched rainforest or on a coral reef, life feels complete, all encompassing, as God intended."

"I know what you mean," I agree. "That completeness somehow makes me feel more whole and at peace."

"That's good," replies Elin. "People need to respect and care for animals and the environment we all live in. The Earth needs our care more than ever and requires love and respect, otherwise the future of our planet is not optimistic. Living in harmony and balance is the way forward.

"It is so sad that so many animals are endangered and their habitats are being so rapidly destroyed. Time is running out and humanity needs to change its incessant desire for more and more things and processed food. It needs to reduce population growth to turn back the clock to a time where there was greater balance. Sustainability must be the way.

"Complex issues," I muse, while placing berries in the basket. "On TV I've seen stories about forests being knocked down all over the world and about endangered species and threatened reefs. It all seems hopeless."

"It can," says Elin, "but there are lots of good people and organisations working to save nature and species. There is some hope."

"We hear a lot more bad stories than good ones. The saddest thing I've seen is the baby orphan orangutans in Malaysia coming out of the knocked down forest without their mothers."

"Yes, that's terrible," agrees Elin. "Malaysian and Indonesian farmers are knocking down the forest to develop palm plantations to produce palm oil used to make processed food, like biscuits. It might help if there was not such a market for palm oil. It's so sad to see those baby orangutans. There is something in the eyes of an orangutan—like a deep knowing, wisdom and seemingly, sadness. That is a pitiful example of things happening all over the world. The world is much less rich without its amazing animals. Can you imagine a world without elephants, rhinoceros, big cats, dolphins or whales?"

"No, I can't. I don't like to think of that happening."

"For many species, it is the final hour. There are many people trying to save them, but it's a very uphill task." Elin picks some hard to reach berries, adding impetus to her comment.

"I imagine it to be so," I reflect, "and so complex in many places, with local people, governments, farmers, business people, hunters and poachers to deal with."

"True, but there has to be some optimism, as otherwise nothing might happen to try to save nature and species. Seeing planet Earth from space is an amazing and beautiful sight and it seems unbelievable that man has wrought so much destruction upon her.

"In nature, where man's footprint has been minimal, there is a feeling of rightness, completeness, harmony and balance. In a green rainforest amongst the tall trees, moss, emerald lichens, ferns, trickling water, birds rustling through the undergrowth—a human may feel the harmony and completeness of life there, how God intended it to be. We want to feel that harmony and completeness within ourselves. The world is broken as nature is broken and so too is humanity.

"Time is running out and we need to reduce global warming, stop deforestation and the loss of habitat, reduce pollution, overfishing, soil erosion and other environmental disasters. We need to act now if there is to be any future for Earth's creatures and humanity.

"There needs to be a return to a feminine approach of nurturing. The Earth needs our love and care as much as our children do. We need to try and live harmoniously within nature's balance which will take great effort on the part of governments, miners, manufacturers, forest managers, fishers, farmers and all consumers.

"Masculine energy and population growth have created ongoing and growing materialism, greed, wars and environmental destruction. There is no way forward except a return to feminine energy and simplicity to recover what has been lost.

"With a return to balance the Earth may recover and become the place of great health and beauty, God's garden, which she was created to be."

"Beautiful words, Elin," I compliment her, "and so much wisdom. I hope there will be more positive change."

"There will be," assures Elin. "I can feel it."

Her basket is almost full and darkness approaches. We bid each other farewell.

I meander through nature, loving it and hoping for good things in its future.

Chapter Ten

MYA'S FUTURE

Today I had the day off and Mum and Dad took me to look at the other schools and meet with the Year 9 advisors. I liked the small, country, private school which has equine studies, but it would be a long trip on the bus and, like my current school, there are only a small number of students in each year. I don't want to end up in the same situation again. The local high school is huge and does seem impersonal, but there are heaps of kids there and the rules don't seem to be too strict. They don't mind if I go away to the mountains with my family. At my school, they made a huge fuss about this when the principal received the note explaining my absence. With it in hand, he talked to the vice-principal in the schoolyard. It was as if I had committed the greatest sin, but that holiday is a regular highlight of my year. The French teacher lectured the class about how lucky we were to be at that school and how important education is. I wanted to sink into the floorboards. Last year

I had to stay at my grandparent's house feeling lonely and forlorn. Well, it's good to know the high school teachers wouldn't mind.

The high school is not nearly as attractive as my current school. The old, red brick building at the front is imposing. Behind it are double-storey brick veneer buildings in dry grounds, lots of cement and kids everywhere. My school has lovely gardens, lots of green areas, old European trees and white single-storey buildings. The high school doesn't offer the same sporting and cultural opportunities, but I guess you can't have everything. There are girls there from my primary school, so at least I would know people when I start. "Don't rush your decision," said Mum. "You still have a few weeks to decide."

I liked the Year 9 advisors—both men seemed caring and interested in their students. Some thinking ahead.

This afternoon I saddle Goldie up and ride my golden, dappled mare through the sun-drenched, dappled forest with golden Sefton trailing behind. All very golden.

Elin is standing beside the rock when I reach my destination. "What a lovely horse," she says, patting Goldie's neck.

"Yes, she is," I agree, as I dismount and tie her to a small mountain ash. Sefton frolics beside the stream.

"How was your day today?" asks Elin, strangely in a golden dress.

"Eventful," I reply. "Mum and Dad took me to the two possible schools I might start at next term. Now I have to make a decision."

"I'm glad you've finally done that. Do you mind if I talk a little about decision making today, Mya?" queries Elin, as she climbs onto the rock.

"Not at all. Perfect timing," I respond, as I sit down on the smaller rock.

"When you have a decision to make it is useful to write down the potential alternative outcomes of the decision and the possible negative, neutral and positive impacts. With these in mind the decision will be easier."

"That might help," I reflect. "It is confusing as there are negative and positive aspects to each school."

Elin nods in agreement, "When a decision has to be made, especially those of a pivotal nature, take your time. Rushed decisions don't always lead to ideal outcomes.

"If emotions are strongly involved, try to stand back from them and see the situation as clearly as possible.

"Write down the alternatives and different impacts. The right choice should arise like a new leaf unfurling, ready to face its new life, unfettered by confusion."

"I will try that," I respond. "It all seems a bit overwhelming."

"You have time."

"I know. Another part of it is the subjects available. At the moment my electives are history, agriculture, French and art. I love all these subjects but cannot continue with them all at both schools. The country school has French but the high school doesn't. Agriculture and art are on the same line at the high school, and at the other school the choices are more complicated because of equine studies being thrown into the equation."

"That's difficult," reflects Elin. "Subject choice is important as it sets the beginning of your academic pathway. Choose subjects that resonate with your soul—that interest you, that you are good at, that allow your creative fire to burn. Of course, you can change later, but having that awareness in your decision making at subject choice time will be of great benefit now and in the future."

"The subjects I'm doing now fit those criteria. I wish I didn't have to give up any of them, but it's not a perfect world and at the moment friendship is a high priority. I want to feel accepted and comfortable at school."

"Yes, at your age that is extremely important. Well, as I said, think slowly and carefully."

"I'll try to do that. I have time to think. I'm not doing much homework or study at the moment as there seems no point to it."

"That's understandable. In your future, work as hard as you can at school as there will be benefits later on, but don't let it hamper your happiness and peace of mind. If the burden becomes too much to bear, seek counselling, change subjects, repeat, or maybe alter your goals so they don't push you beyond your limits.

"When studying, a good idea is to study for 50 minutes and then take a break for 10 minutes doing something totally different, like a walk outside or tidying your room. You will return fresh and ready to learn some more."

"I do get tired studying, and sometimes I lose my concentration."

"Just set reasonable goals. When goal setting, it can be beneficial to break down the process of reaching the goal into little steps so you progress slowly and steadily towards your desired outcome. Writing those things down is helpful to refer back to and keep on track. Writing your goals on a card and keeping it somewhere prominent may inspire you."

"That is very practical and useful advice Elin. Thank you."

"You are welcome, Mya. I know this is early days, but do you think about what you want to do after completing high school?"

"Well, it hasn't been on my mind lately, but I'd love to be a writer or an artist. I know they are difficult and competitive areas to pursue. Mum and Dad say I'll never have any money and I need to think of a more practical career to fall back on. They definitely want Ben and I to go to university. They value education."

"That's a good thing," observes Elin. "Hold onto your dreams. They are important and can sustain you. Don't give up on your dreams, dear Mya."

"I'll try not to."

"When students have completed their school studies it may be useful for them to get an apprenticeship, go to TAFE[2], college or university. It is a competitive world out there and qualifications count. Of course, it is not essential, but it may be beneficial to have that backstop."

"That's exactly what Mum and Dad think, and as they both went to uni they want us to do that too, but I know TAFE has some great art courses."

"Yes, there are lots of options out there."

---

[2] Technical and Further Education (Australia)

"Some kids find thinking about the future depressing. All we hear about is environmental doom and gloom, global warming, violence on many levels, terrible wars, terrorism and high youth unemployment."

"That's understandable. To immunise yourself against that, it may be best not to watch too much television or read too many articles in the newspapers or on the internet. You need to have hope and optimism for the future. During World War II it must have felt like hell on Earth, but when it finally ended, countries and people eventually recovered, though many were scarred for life. One old man once told me that you should try to look after yourself and your immediate environment and not worry too much about problems beyond your control. That may be helpful advice when you are young. However, young people can be creative and adaptable and can make their own opportunities. They are standing up now and letting their thoughts and feelings be heard by adults and governments. As I said before, as you work towards your dreams, and as long as it feels right, you will be amazed at times how life seems to be magical and flow effortlessly. You are living as you should and your energy is working well for you. The right people, opportunities and places will arise as needed and your light will shine."

"I love that idea," I compliment Elin.

"It helps me," she replies, "as does spirituality. My faith gives me strength. Spirituality can be fostered in young people. They can pray, create, meditate and connect to God, and through that connection they are beings of light illuminating the world. You said you go to a youth group, Mya?"

"Yes, sometimes."

"During teenage years, young people may begin seeking the spirit within and God surrounding all that is. Through joining religious or spiritual groups they may explore this aspect further and rejoice in their faith in God.

"Prayer, meditation, reading spiritual books, ritual and communing in nature may all enhance the spiritual life. As a person discovers the God within and around her, she will become more composed, peaceful, aware and happy.

"Whilst meeting like-minded souls, life may be enriched as the soul's journey is enhanced. As your spiritual bloom blossoms, Mya, God will be smiling."

"Lovely thought," I reflect.

Goldie is becoming a little agitated, stamping at her tree, and Sefton is in hot pursuit of a rabbit, in usual Sefton fashion. "I think they're telling me something."

"Yes, time to go dear girl."

A brief hug, I thank Elin and we say goodbye as I untie Goldie. I mount up, call Sefton and trot home through the glimmering forest with renewed strength and hope.

Chapter Eleven

CHALLENGES

I'm getting through the days at school. Grace often meets up with me at recess to see how I'm going. I reassure her that I'm getting better.

Emma is a sweet girl in Year 7 with long, red hair, hazel eyes, a petite nose and very fair skin. She is a bit of a loner, like me, and is also quiet and sensitive. Today, at lunchtime, I saw a couple of the dominant and popular Year 7 girls pull her plaits and taunt her with, "Emma, Emma, you're too clever." She is gifted academically. Emma ran off to the locker room with tears pouring down her china-doll cheeks and me in pursuit.

"Oh, you poor thing." I gave Emma a hug, the shoe on the other foot. "Don't worry about what those girls are saying. You are beautiful, smart and talented. I know exactly what you are going through."

"Thank you, Mya," said Emma, just managing to get some words out between sobs. "Those girls are hard to deal with. I don't know what to do."

"For a start, maybe talk to one of the teachers and the school counsellor," I suggested.

"I guess so," replied Emma, "but that could make things worse."

"Well, how about we just go and see Mrs. Bishop? She is good to talk to and then at least someone will know what's going on."

"Okay," agreed Emma, somewhat reluctantly.

We went to see the old history teacher in her classroom. She listened attentively and was very concerned. She said she would organise for Emma to see the school counsellor and some disciplinary action for the girls involved. Emma, despite being disinclined, accepted those things. The bell went for afternoon classes. "Try not to worry Emma. You're not alone."

"Thank you, Mya. It's good to know that."

We returned to the locker room and I kept an eye on the Year 7 area to ensure no further bullying would be missed. Everything was fairly orderly. I waited outside the door with books in hand. Emma walked out. "I'll be thinking of you Emma."

"It's good to know someone understands," she replied sweetly.

"I'll see you soon." We departed in opposite directions. It made me feel so sad to see such a gentle girl being treated like that. Kids can be so mean.

I meander through the forest with Sefton exploring. Whispit suddenly jumps out from behind a log, grabbing my leg with his elegant paw. "Oh, you naughty boy," I scold, as I pick the cat up and give him a little hug. I prefer him not to come, but he has obviously been on our trail, and we have gone too far now.

Elin is leaning against the rock. She spies my new companion. "What an unusual cat," she observes.

"I know. If Whispit was human, he would be termed eccentric. He does lots of weird things and I think he thinks he is a dog. He likes to follow me everywhere and seems to enjoy surprising me, jumping into my arms from hidden places or onto the horses backs."

"What breed is he?"

"An Oriental, similar to a Siamese. He's a character."

"I can see that," says Elin, as Whispit does his crisscrossed, pigeon-toed walk and then jumps into her arms, simultaneously voicing his whiney meow. She laughs and gives him a pat. "You're a lovely boy, Whispit."

Stroking his cheek with the cat now purring, Elin suggests we sit on our rocks.

I tell her of today's incident, how upsetting it was for Emma and for me as I tried to console her.

"I'm sorry to hear about that, Mya. Bullying is a terribly destructive problem."

"I know. It was sad to see such a sweet girl being treated like that."

"Yes, understandably. I mentioned empathy earlier. It is desirable for parents and teachers to teach children about empathy. They need to become aware that whatever they say or do to another human being has an effect. They need to be encouraged to put themselves in the position of the other person and to imagine how he would feel as a result of their words or actions. With empathy and greater awareness, the world would become a more loving and caring place. It is beneficial that children have the same regard for all animals and nature—to care for all of God's Earth and her creatures."

"I wish it could be like that," I sigh, "but the reality of school is far from it."

"I know," agrees Elin. "Another important thing is that parents maintain vigilance regarding their child's emotional wellbeing. If they notice a change, they need to talk to her, and then maybe her teachers, school counsellor or principal. If bullying is occurring, prompt action needs to be taken.

"Vigilance is required regarding internet and mobile phone use. Parents need to speak with their child and be a part of social networking. Communication and awareness will help greatly in this area.

"Yes, bullying happens a lot through the internet and phones," I observe. "It has even led some kids to suicide. It's terrible."

"Yes, the very ugly impact of technology," says Elin. "These things need to be addressed and discussed openly to reduce bullying and its negative consequences. I will also add that the bully needs to develop empathy and put themselves in their victim's shoes. It is beneficial for the bully to seek help from a counsellor, and then he too, may move forward in his life."

"It might be very difficult to get a bully to do that," I respond.

"True, but such action may have to be enforced, and it may be surprising to see the bully turn around and maybe even become somewhat sensitive."

"Sensitive," I sigh. "Mum and Dad say I'm too sensitive and I know poor Emma is too."

"That's a positive thing," reflects Elin. "You and Emma have already developed empathy. This cultivates your sensitivity. It is good to be aware and sensitive towards the wellbeing of your friends, other kids, family, teachers and elders. Treating others with dignity and respect as well as animals and the environment may enhance the growth of your soul."

"I hope so," I discern, "but my sensitivity has caused me some problems so far."

"You see it like that now. However, in the long-run, as you grow older and look back on things, you will be glad to have been sensitive and how it has led to greater understanding, knowledge and appreciation of life. It is something you can be thankful for. Thankfulness or gratitude is very useful in life. I'm always thanking God for my healthy body, my family, friends, opportunities as they arise, my talents, meeting you, Mya, the nature that surrounds us. Gratitude helps me appreciate my life and everything about it."

"I do that sometimes," I reply, "but not so much lately. When you experience bullying, or see others in that situation, it's hard to feel gratitude."

"I understand that," says Elin, "but things are getting better for you and I'm sure they will for Emma too."

"I hope so."

"I'm glad you didn't acquiesce to those girls trying to get you to smoke, Mya. Life is a gift, as is your body, which also requires respect and care. Cigarettes, drugs and alcohol, beyond moderation, harm your body and diminish your soul's progress."

"Hmm," I nod. "Some people think smoking is cool, but I think it's disgusting, and I have no desire to use drugs or drink at this stage."

"That's good," commends Elin. "Things may change when you are older. As a young adult you may tend to rush into life at full force, wanting to taste all it has to offer with gusto, but remember balance—through diet, exercise, limiting undesirable substances and nurturing your spiritual life. Balance gives equanimity to your soul, enhancing your spiritual journey.

"Cigarettes, drugs and alcohol diminish you and cloud your clarity, cutting you off from a soulful life."

"Well I want a soulful life," I respond. "At least I know that."

"Excellent, Mya. Was there anything else you wanted to talk about this evening?"

"Well, there is one other girl at school who concerns me. She's in Year 10 and looks skeletal. She only eats an apple for lunch. She doesn't appear to be happy and she definitely looks unhealthy. I don't know her, but I think something is wrong."

"Ah, that sounds like anorexia. The girl must be suffering a lot. I'm not sure about the whole picture concerning anorexia, but I've heard brain chemistry plays a role. I feel also that the media and fashion industry have created the *ideal* image of the thin, athletic body, but this is unnatural. A girl should aim for her suitable body weight as advised by her doctor. It is what is on the inside that counts, the shining human spirit. It is wise to be healthy through a balanced diet and exercise but not to let this snowball into anorexia and bulimia—terrible diseases of the modern western world. Skeletal images are shocking—there is no beauty in that. People need to seek help early if they are heading that way, or assist others who may need to do so. It is the real person inside that counts, and people need to love themselves and remember that God loves them and is waiting for their love.

"Do you think the girl is getting any assistance with her condition?" asks Elin.

"Going on how she looks and acts, maybe not," I reply.

"Maybe you could mention it to the school counsellor or the history teacher to get things rolling."

"Maybe, but I don't know the girl. They might think it's weird."

"No, they won't. They will think you are being a mature and caring girl."

"Hmm, possibly. At the other end of the spectrum, there's a boy in my year whose parents own a fish and chip shop. He's a big boy. He hates exercise and really struggles with PE and sport."

"That's another common problem," says Elin. "Obesity is a huge and growing problem in the world. Processed foods and lack of exercise contribute to this. If a person is overweight, he needs to see his doctor regarding diet and exercise and she will help put in place a plan to achieve his ideal weight and maintain it. It can be extremely difficult, but worth it in the long run, as when a person feels lighter, he may feel more confident and have more energy to pursue his goals and dreams."

"You always talk about goals and dreams," I observe.

"They are important," replies Elin. "They help to keep you hopeful, optimistic, motivated and disciplined—all positive aspects in a soulful life."

"Can you explain a bit more what you mean by a soulful life?" I ask my wise teacher.

"Well, a life without God may be meaningful to a human being, but a life with God is enriched and directed. Such a human being becomes fulfilled, at peace and cultivates the nourishment of her soul.

"The spiritual life encompasses dedication and faith in God. It embodies a loving human who cares for others, animals and nature. He finds his talents and shares them with the world to make it a better place. He does the best he can in whatever circumstances he finds himself in while considering the needs and desires of those around him. He is aware of himself as a spiritual being, here to learn and help others. He pays attention to details and tries to live a harmonious existence with gratitude."

"That sound beautiful," I reflect, "and it's a great guidepost."

"I hope so," says Elin, quietly, gently.

A wind is lifting—a storm brewing—time for our farewells. Yet again, I have much to think about as I wander home with Whispit trotting behind me and Sefton scampering ahead, and very practical ideas too.

Chapter Twelve

A SOLUTION

Mum cooks bacon and eggs for breakfast. As Dad pours the orange juice he asks, "Have you decided which school you want to go to, Mya?"

"I've been really thinking it over and wrote down the pros and cons of going to each school. I think the high school is the best option."

"Are you sure? The other school seems like a very nice environment."

"I know, but my school also seems like that. You can't always judge by appearances."

"Very true," agrees Mum, as she serves our breakfast, "but what about the opportunity to do equine studies?"

"That does sound great, but I'm going to Pony Club and read books and online articles. I can learn that way and I don't really want to give up any of my current subjects."

"That's understandable," says Mum, "but you are going to have to change them. You probably can't continue with French and will have to choose between art and agriculture."

"That's very difficult, but I definitely don't want to stay where I am. The reasons I want to go to the high school are that it's not so far on the bus, I already know lots of kids there and as it's such a large school, I should find people that I have things in common with."

"That's right, Mya," says Dad. "We just want you to be sure about it and we really want you to be happy."

"Thanks Dad." I go to his chair and give him a hug. He is usually so busy with work and the farm that he doesn't pay much attention to the details of our lives, but when it comes to pivotal decisions, he is always supportive and puts forward his thoughts.

"Well, we'll have to give notice at your school in a week's time," says Mum, "and we'll go and see the Year 9 advisor at the high school, enroll you and sort out your subjects."

"Okay, thanks Mum."

Today I feel lighter at school, but I am just pushing through my time here—it all seems pointless.

At recess I see Emma playing handball with a group of boys and girls. She smiles and waves hello. She seems much better.

Grace asks me what my plans are and she is glad I've made a decision. "That school should be much better for you, Mya."

"I hope so," I reply.

After my history class I hang back and mention the thin girl to my lovely teacher. She says she will talk to the school counsellor about it.

Waiting for the bus can be unbearable. I don't want to be here anyway, and I have to be here for half an hour longer. Watch that clock—come on 4:00 p.m.

After my chores, Sefton and I head down the path. Elin is not at the rock or picking berries. "Unusual," I think to myself. "She must have had something else to do."

I decide to just sit on the rock, enjoy nature and reflect—thinking of God and oneness.

GOD

God is in me

Around me

In you

Around you

In everything, around everything

God connects

Creates meaning

My temple is in the desert

My church is on the mountain

My synagogue is by the river bank

My mosque touches the ocean

In Nature I find God

In Stillness, Simplicity

And my love pours forth

Connecting me, feeling I am in God and God is in me

Oneness, available to all humanity—ready to be united in the love of one God who does not discriminate

A misty rain falls, pulling me out of my reverie. The evenings are becoming cooler. I call Sefton and we walk home briskly as a full moon peaks above the horizon.

Chapter Thirteen

FOR YOUNG ADULTS

Long one. Sorry.

After school I finish my chores quickly and then saddle up Casper. The cheeky pony needs some work and Ben hasn't been interested in riding recently. Casper doesn't want to leave home, but once I'm out on the reserve he happily walks along with ears pricked forward. Sefton follows, diverting here and there to chase rabbits or explore.

Elin is leaning against the rock. She turns and smiles a friendly greeting, "Hello, Mya."

"Hi, Elin."

"What a lovely pony."

"Sometimes lovely. He's a lazy boy. Casper belongs to Ben and he hasn't been wanting to ride lately, so I decided to give his pony some work."

Elin gives Casper a pat on the neck as I dismount. "I love horses," she says. "They are so beautiful and such sensitive creatures."

"Yes, they are very aware of emotions," I reply, "and sometimes I think they can tell what I'm thinking too. They mean everything to me. I'm glad they can be a part of my life."

"Yes, that is a fortunate thing... I couldn't get here yesterday because I went to town to buy vegetable seedlings for my winter garden which I needed to plant last night on the full moon." Elin is such an interesting mix of ethereal and earthy. It almost seems contradictory, but to me she seems to be a perfectly balanced human.

"I missed you, but I meditated on the rock. I felt the stillness within me and around me, and felt connected to God," I reveal, as I tie Casper to a small wattle tree which he proceeds to munch on.

"Good girl," Elin compliments me, and then asks, "Now, how is Emma?"

"She seems much better. She's been playing handball with a group of friendly kids."

"Excellent, and did you talk to the counsellor about the girl in Year 10?"

"No, but I did mention her to my history teacher who said she would talk to the counsellor."

"That's good," reflects Elin. "And how is your decision-making progressing about which school you want to go to?"

"Well, I did that thing you suggested of writing down the pros and cons of each school and it's possible positive and negative aspects and eventually decided on the high school as it's a much shorter bus trip, I know kids there and it's a much bigger school, so I should find people there I have things in common with."

"Great, Mya. I'm glad you've reached a decision. It's a shame about your subjects though."

"I know, especially having to choose between agriculture and art as I love both of them. French has to go and it looks like I'll be doing German instead."

"Multilingual Mya," laughs Elin.

"Mumbling, tongue-twisted Mya more likely."

More tinkling laughter. "Art or agriculture. Hmm, I would have trouble deciding which one to do too. I feel passionate about both. Everyone needs something to be passionate about, to enliven the fire in their soul. If an individual doesn't have a passion, it is useful to seek one out, to nurture it and there will be rewards and happiness."

"Yes," I agree, "passion is important. I need to think a bit more about that decision."

We are both sitting on the rock now, and Elin has resumed teacher mode. "I might jump ahead a bit, if that's okay by you, Mya, and talk about some things that relate to your life when you're older. It may be beneficial for you to write them down in your journal so you've got that to refer back to."

"Okay. I'm open to hearing any of your insights Elin. It's all been very useful so far."

"Thank you. I might start with work. Ideally, you would be in a job you love, something that comes naturally to you, so everything else falls into place. Otherwise, take steps to change by studying, volunteering or taking a part-time job in the preferred field. Whatever gifts you have, try to use them to help others. Try to do what makes you happy."

"I'll keep that in mind."

"As a young adult, you may be driven to obtain more and more material objects," continues Elin, "but in the end, they can enslave you. People spend so much time caring for these objects they can distract them from the spiritual journey and spending quality time with others.

"The richest man on Earth is unlikely to be the happiest. People with great riches often have great problems and fall prey to the darkest side of life—drug and alcohol abuse, gambling and psychological problems. This is so often seen amongst the famous—musicians and actors. They have all the money in the world and fame, which is not necessarily so desirable. They have opportunities abounding, but they are so often victims of their own lifestyles and psychological capacity to cope.

"Be wary of desiring fame as it is not always the golden pathway painted by the media.

"Simplicity can lead to happiness, things in moderation and time for a soulful life."

"I like that idea about simplicity," I reflect. "Mum and Dad work hard and have money, but they also like the principle of simplicity and our lives aren't crowded with material objects and gadgets."

"That's good, Mya. Money is positive in that it is a form of energy for exchange. It needs to keep moving, but some people use it for negative pursuits, such as gambling, which can cut them off from the spiritual life and can be very destructive when it becomes an addiction. Poker machines were designed to lure people in and the chance of winning a decent amount of money is close to zilch. Individuals should not be influenced by others to follow this path as it may harm them and those close to them. If someone fails and falls down here, he should seek counselling and hopefully be able to overcome this urge."

"I know that can be a terrible problem," I reply. "There's always old people playing those poker machines at the pub. It seems so mindless and I actually find the lights and music aggravating. It's hard for me to understand how people can get addicted to them."

"Well, they might have won a good prize once or may have seen someone else do so and they're chasing that, or their lives are empty and gambling helps fill the void. If they were more spiritually inclined and looked beyond the veneer of everyday life, they probably wouldn't have such a desire. Drinking and drug problems can be caused by similar things."

"Yes, that can be terrible. One of Dad's friends has a drinking and a gambling problem and he ended up losing his job, his marriage and his house as a result."

"Hmm, it's best to nip those problems in the bud, before that terrible destruction occurs. Counselling helps, as does some form of control of budgeting. That leads into some discussion of relationships. As a young adult, relationships can be very exciting—exploring life with another human is enriching and can be life and soul enhancing, but discernment is necessary. If you feel drained on any level by a relationship and after attempts to solve a lack of harmony fail, it may be best to end the relationship.

"If the other person is leading you down a destructive path of dark activity, that may be a signal to end the relationship. Seek counselling, try whatever you can, but don't let a relationship diminish you or your light-filled journey towards God.

"If you experience abuse on any level, seek help. No one deserves this. Make sure you let others know what is going on and don't stay where you or your future children may be harmed.

"Sometimes a relationship may sour with weariness, but try to remember what drew you to that person in the first place and relive that admiration. Take out special time together at a restaurant, on a picnic, a walk in the mountains and remember why you love that man or woman beside you and nourish the partnership that you share. Life is a ride of ups and downs and through them you will grow."

"Yes, well I've just been through a down," I observe.

"True, and the up is approaching, dear Mya. You have found a solution to your problem and hopefully things will be smoother for you soon. Acceptance is important in life in general. Things will not always be as you desire. If you are not happy in a situation, try to accept it. Take steps to change and have patience. To keep on an even keel, useful tools are acceptance and patience."

"I'm slowly learning that."

"Not so slowly," says Elin. "It might seem like I'm jumping all over the place, but I want to cover a few more things this evening that will stand you in good stead as you grow older. Illness is one of those. Sometimes it strikes and it may take a long time to recover, sometimes a lifetime.

"Seek all the medical help you can, try alternative methods and look at your diet and lifestyle. It can be difficult to rest, but that may be your only choice, and it may be an opportunity for spiritual growth through reading, prayer and meditation.

"Acceptance helps. If you can't change a situation, acceptance leads to peace of mind and a more positive outlook and strength to cope."

"I get a lot of colds and flus and I find it frustrating sometimes. I can see Ben and Craig playing outside and wish I could get out there and do something too. I'll try to be more accepting next time."

"It does seem to help," responds Elin. "As does having gratitude. Sometimes, when life seems so difficult and you are in a situation that seems not so great for you, having gratitude can be helpful. You can be grateful for your family, friends, pets, having a roof over your head (hopefully), food on the table, safety, a beautiful sunset and leading a spiritually inspired life. Appreciating the little things in your life can be beneficial and healing for your soul."

I nod in agreement.

"Another topic I want to cover is judgement. As you proceed through life you may judge yourself in terms of your progress—whether it be academic, materially, career success, even spiritually—and you may do so in terms of others' attainments. If you have not reached a certain goal by a certain time you may be self-punishing which may diminish your feelings of self-worth. Don't judge yourself in negative terms—just keep moving steadily forward, at times stopping and taking things in, possibly sliding back a little, but like the tortoise, you will get there in the end, somehow. Possibly your goals may change which alters the canvas of your life.

"Life is like a river, meandering this way and that. Sometimes the water may pause at a bend, or in a lake, but eventually it reaches the ocean.

"Judging others is a waste of time and energy. They are living a life they have chosen and judgement has no point.

"Envy is also of little use. Being at peace with where you are and your destination is the soulful way.

"Do the best that you can in the circumstances you find yourself in. Don't punish yourself if you fall short of expectations."

"Thank you, Elin. That all makes lots of sense."

"I hope so. What about travel, Mya? Do you have any desire to do so?"

"Oh yes, I'd love to go to Nepal, especially as I was made there."

"I hope you get there," chuckles Elin. "It is a beautiful country. Travel is a great way to open the mind and learn of the variety of life. Through seeing other ways of being with awareness and sensitivity you will be nourished on a soul level. It will also help with developing empathy. You may learn greater respect and love for nature as displayed by people living close to her, such as the Mongolian nomads or Amazon Indians. These people know how important it is to care for the environment and their lives are entwined within it."

"Yes, I've seen documentaries about that," I respond. "We can learn a lot from indigenous people around the world."

"Very true," acknowledges Elin. She pauses, then says, "Now for a totally different subject, again relevant as you grow older."

"I'm ready," I reply.

"Do you hope to have children one day, Mya?"

"Yes, maybe just two," I smile, shyly.

"Well, I want to talk a little about that as there is a trend in the western world towards parenting later in life and some couples face great disappointment if they are unable to have children. If you desire children, take care not to leave it until it is too late. This trend has left many women childless with feelings of grief and loss for the unborn child and mother they will never be. If this desire is strong within you, you need to be planning by 32 if everything is well with you and your partner on a gynaecological level.

"If you find yourself childless and you didn't desire this outcome and there is no opportunity for adoption, there may be a big hole in your life that you hoped to be filled with nurturing your children and their cries and laughter.

"If so, seek counselling as your boat's anchor has become stuck in some dark sludge that can be difficult to sail out of, but once you do so you may be able to find peace with this situation. You can be grateful for your relationship, other children in your life, peace and quiet for study, prayer, contemplation and meditation, time for pursuit of your own interests or travel—endless possibilities and freedom.

"You need to channel your energy in other ways—through work, relationships of all types, charity work, creative pursuits. There are so many opportunities, and this time, your energy needs to be put to good use elsewhere than having children. This is a great opportunity for soulful work and a soulful life."

"Some of our closest family friends don't have children," I reveal, "and they are very content people. We love going to visit them on their farms and they are all very interested in Ben and I. Some of my happiest memories are of those visits."

"That's very good, Mya. Now for another challenging topic in the same vein. Miscarriage is a natural process and it's normal to feel grief and loss for the baby. If you experience miscarriage, don't be hard on yourself, and take time to nurture yourself and heal. Take it slowly and lovingly and seek counselling if you are overwhelmed."

"That would be so difficult," I observe. "Mum had a miscarriage between Ben and I and she said it was a very sad and challenging time."

"It can be," affirms Elin. "That's why it's important for parents to be gentle with themselves and take time to heal."

"Mm."

"Now I want to talk about stay-at-home mums and dads. They are doing a wonderful job. Bringing up children in a safe, loving and soul-filled way is one of the most important jobs on Earth. If you become a stay-at-home mum, if at all possible, put aside some special time each week just for you, whether it be a dance class, playing sport, coffee with a friend or walking in a forest—something that nourishes your soul."

"A couple of my friends have stay-at-home mums and sometimes I feel envious. They have cakes and pikelets waiting for them when they get home from school and they don't have many chores to do. Sometimes I feel like I'm Ben's mum."

"Well, you're learning lots of skills and about responsibility which will benefit you later in life," says Elin.

"I guess so," I agree, but not totally convinced. "Sometimes I have to do cleaning as well because Mum and Dad are so busy."

"Ah, that brings me to the next topic—home is your temple. Wherever you live it is your temple, whether it be a tent, a caravan, an apartment, a cabin or a house. As you keep it clean and ordered there will be space in your mind and heart. Clutter creates confusion and clouds the mind.

"From time-to-time, cleaning out the home—ridding yourself of the unnecessary—is cleansing on all levels, and may involve some release of the past.

"As you care for your home, your temple, you care for your soul. Cleaning the home can be loving, a ritual and a meditation. Humans have been dusting, sweeping, mopping and gardening for millennia. As you do these things you may feel connected to the ancient, the simple, the humble—to the continuity of human life. As you put your hands in the soil you may feel connected to the Earth and all that is. Tickle the Earth and make her laugh."

"I know what you mean," I chortle. "When I do gardening, I feel grounded and when I do cleaning, I do find it to be meditative if I'm in the right frame of mind. Mum's got a gorgeous picture of an old Nepalese woman in bright clothes and a headscarf sweeping the cobble stones outside her stone house with a small straw broom which reminds me of a witch's broom. She looks so sweet, happy and humble as she is doing this task. Mum says the people in those less developed countries often seem much happier without the materialism of the western world. Family and spirituality are important to them and just living in tune with the seasons and nature's rhythms allows them to have a content and meaningful existence. Life seems so complicated here sometimes."

"Yes, but it doesn't have to be," replies Elin. "Simplicity is a key to the door of leading a soulful life."

"Mm," I nod in agreement.

"The picture of the old Nepalese woman sounds beautiful. That brings me to the topic of ageing. In western society there is so much focus on youthful looks, beauty and fashion, it can create fear and dread of ageing, but this is a natural process. The gradual lining of the face and greying of the hair would be better relished as the time approaches of greater freedom and time to pursue interests and spiritual growth.

"In relationships, it can be a great time of sharing and peace. It may be the time to finally achieve unfulfilled dreams. It may be the time to celebrate simplicity and rejoice in the beauty of the garden you have created or a painting you have finally painted. It is a time to enjoy your family and friends at a slower pace. It is a gift to be embraced."

"I cherish my grandparents and godmother," I tell Elin. "They are leading happy lives. None of them are in nursing homes. Nan is a great gardener and cook. She makes the best chicken pie, chocolate éclairs, Spanish cream, crème caramel and Belgian cakes. At Christmas, Ben and I and all our cousins eat strawberry ice cream and peppermint-creams, sitting out in Nan's garden under strings of coloured lights strung from a huge Liquid Amber tree. It's so much fun. Bella, my godmother, is also a great gardener. She didn't have any children and she is a very wise and content woman. The older people in my life are great role-models, but I know what you mean about there being a fear and dread of ageing. Some young people don't want anything to do with older people and some families push their elderly relatives into nursing homes."

"True," agrees Elin. "Generally, there is a lack of respect for the elderly in modern, western culture. Not so in Asia or India, where the elderly are revered and cared for within the family. This needs to be turned around. We need to love, care for and respect the elderly—they are a wealth of knowledge and potential teachers—not just the faceless old to be pushed into retirement villages and nursing homes to await their death."

"Yes, it can be a sad situation for some elderly people," I reply.

"I know. That picture you described moved me onto different topics. I just want to cover two more things this evening. One is regarding singles. You may desire a relationship, or you may be happy alone. Either way, your time alone is a time of great freedom as you make choices, plans and pursue dreams. You have a great capacity to cultivate a soulful life and live in harmony with God's love.

"If you desire a relationship, it may arise at the most unexpected place and time. Cherish your alone time. It can be very special."

"I know that," I acknowledge. "I have been forced to have a lot of alone time, but most of the time I enjoy it."

"That's great, Mya. The final topic this evening is spirituality for young adults. By now you may be aware of the listener behind the thoughts— the observer of your mind. The stillness beyond is where you can spend time in meditation, through creativity, sports, in the natural world or through nowness in such simple things as watching the water from the hose touch the garden, without thoughts intruding. The more practice the better and greater harmony will enter your life on all levels. It will also create greater harmony between humans and a more peaceful world."

"I have an inkling of what you mean about the listener behind the thoughts," I observe, "that more pure part of us, the soul part I guess."

"Exactly, dear girl. You are an excellent student."

"They don't think that at school at the moment."

"Well at this school you get 10 out of 10."

"That's pretty good," I beam shyly, adding, "thanks to you being an excellent teacher."

"Oh no," replies Elin humbly, shaking her head. "I'm just passing on what I have learnt and you were in exactly the right place—physically, mentally, emotionally and spiritually—ready like a dry sea sponge waiting to soak up some salty water. It was our destiny to meet, Mya. I don't think it was just a coincidence. Through me helping you now, later on you are going to go on and help many more people."

"That's hard to imagine at the moment, but the future is unknown."

"True, now it's been a lot for you to take in today and it's late, Mya."

"Mm," I nod. The sun has already set beyond the blue hills. "Thank you so much Elin. You are a treasure."

"More so you," reciprocates my teacher.

A little hug. I untie Casper, call the ever-energetic Sefton, mount up and say goodbye. A farewell wave and I'm off at a trot. Casper is keen to get home and eat some hay.

Tonight, my hand nearly falls off as I write about today's teachings. Goodnight, dear reader.

Chapter Fourteen

MIDDLE AND LATER LIFE

Mum is too busy to ride, and Ben just hasn't been keen lately. Today I ride Zora in the forest. He's only four, a black Welsh Cob gelding. He throws in the odd pig-root, but I can cope with that.

As I round the last corner before the rock, Elin spies this different horse. "Oh, what a handsome big boy."

"Yes, he is. He really needs more work too. I wish I could just stay home and work the horses."

"Remember balance," Elin reminds me.

"I know," I sigh.

Elin strokes the gelding's neck and gives him a little scratch under the chin. "That's Zora's favourite thing," I tell her. "He loves that." I dismount and tie my horse to the slightly ragged wattle tree.

We sit on the rock, listening to the gurgling water. There's smoke in the air. Fire brigades are burning off at the moment.

"As we got onto the subject of the elderly yesterday, I thought I might talk a little more about middle and later life this evening. Is that alright by you, Mya?"

"Of course. I'm open to hearing anything you have to say Elin."

"Thank you. Well, the first thing I want to cover is mid-life crisis. Some people may experience this when they reach middle-age, possibly due to feeling dissatisfied with life. It is advisable for them to seek counselling and find ways to channel their energy into positive pursuits. Taking up a new hobby or sport may help. Changing jobs or finally studying what they have always desired to may also be healing. It may be time for them to take that trip they have planned all their life. They need to be careful not to do anything too drastic as they may regret it later on. They need to think of how their actions may affect their family, friends and work colleagues. It is advisable for them to appreciate what they have, the people around them, and not to take them for granted. This may be a time for them to nourish their spiritual lives."

"A friend of Dad's was supposedly happily married but took off to Queensland with his young personal assistant. A few months later it was all over and he'd lost most of the closest relationships in his life. He wasn't happy."

"Mm, sadly that's the sort of thing that can happen," reflects Elin.

We listen to the water babbling as a light breeze plays with fallen leaves.

"The next topic is children leaving home, which may create a huge void for stay-at-home parents and for those working as well. The home may seem too quiet and lifeless. This is an enormous adjustment for everyone. For parents, it is a time of adjusting to a new relationship with adult children, adapting to a more peaceful life and greater freedom and time on their hands. Relationships between partners may be enriched as they get to know one another again on deeper levels and have more opportunities to explore interests and spiritual growth. With this change, it may also be a time they can reach out to others in need."

I nod, listening attentively, learning, remembering.

"Loss of former work or pursuits during middle or later life may lead to grief and loss or depression. It is advisable to seek counselling and to find other ways to channel energy. Volunteering is an excellent opportunity to help other humans, animals and the environment and add meaning to twilight years. Playing sport or undertaking creative pursuits may add joy to life. There may be opportunities to teach young people something individuals have knowledge of through schools, youth groups, cubs and scouts. It is important to keep the mind and body active and not retire to the couch."

"Oh, I know someone who has retired to the couch," I say. "He's a big man and watches sport all day."

"Not advisable for body, mind and soul," laughs Elin.

"No," I agree.

"Loss of physical abilities is difficult and involves acceptance and letting go," explains Elin. "People need to find doable activities and interests to occupy their minds. It may be a great opportunity for spiritual growth.

"With change on any level, there may be grief and loss. When you experience this, tears are healing and allow the grief to flow, as is counselling and possibly joining a support group. If you have lost a family member or friend, sharing memories is helpful, as is exercise and talking to whoever has passed as if they are still with you. Nowness may be of assistance. Take things slowly, and gradually, you will feel acceptance and peace with this change in your life."

"Hmm," I nod affirmatively.

"For people in the later stages of life, their spiritual life may intensify as they read, pray, contemplate, meditate and maybe teach others what they have learnt."

"Thinking about ageing in those terms, it sounds a lot more positive," I reflect.

"Exactly," agrees Elin. "My final point on this topic is to embrace it. This may be the best period of your life. Enjoy it and make the most of your twilight years."

"I will try to remember that," I reply. "It seems like eons away for me, but older people tell me life gets faster and seems shorter as you grow older."

"Time is strange like that," says Elin. "Do you want to do a quick meditation before you ride home?"

"Okay."

With crossed legs and hands resting on our knees, Elin guides me to concentrate on my breathing, to relax and still my mind, to be aware of the thoughts but to just let them pass. I reach a quiet place, beyond the thoughts, in eternal stillness. I feel a part of the rocks, the stream, the forest, all of Creation. What seems like minutes, is in fact, more than half an hour.

The Currawongs are crying out as they glide through the evening sky. Dark clouds are menacing. The black and white birds know it will rain soon. Hopefully, it will wash the smoke out of the air. Zora begins to stamp impatiently. "I better get going."

"Yes," agrees Elin, as she looks up at the grey sky.

"Thank you, yet again Elin. Ageing is nothing to fear or dread. You have almost made me look forward to it."

"A positive thing." Elin pats Zora as I mount up. "See you soon, Mya."

"You will. Bye, Elin." I wave as I urge Zora forward, wanting to beat the rain home. We canter rhythmically under the mountain ash, smelling rich eucalyptus, feeling alive and happy.

Chapter Fifteen

THE WORLD AS IT IS

Today I decide to walk to the forest with Sefton. After the rain, the vegetation is glistening, alive and green. A wallaby thumps through the undergrowth with Sefton off in hot pursuit, typical Sefton. An earthy, damp, eucalyptus redolence envelopes everything and the air is clear. The smoke has gone.

"Hello, Elin," I greet my teacher.

"Hello, Mya. How are you today?"

"I'm good, and you?"

"I'm well, thank you. I was very pleased with the rain, just what my seedlings need at the moment."

"Yes, everything is washed anew."

"Even you, Mya," smiles Elin.

"Getting there," I reply, quietly.

"Definitely," assures Elin.

We sit on our adjoining rocks. "Today I would like to talk about the world as it is, if that's okay by you, Mya?"

"Yes, that's fine, but a complicated topic and it can seem overwhelming to kids when we think about global warming, environmental destruction, terrorism, wars everywhere, terrible diseases like Ebola, youth unemployment, discrimination—when you think about these things the outlook only seems bleak."

"I can understand that, but remember there are individuals and groups doing great things out there. If it was just totally bleak, everyone would give up, and it is generally human nature to strive to achieve goals or to improve conditions for themselves and their families. There are many people who care deeply about the environment, animals and social issues.

"Masculine energy dominates this world. Too many politicians and business leaders are caught up in ego. There is rampant materialism and greed with too little care for personal wellbeing or that of the environment. The desire for more material possessions such as new model cars and gadgets, new houses and processed food—and population growth—drive onward environmental destruction worldwide which is not without consequence.

"Without empathy, there is a lack of understanding others' ethnicity, culture, tribe, religion, sexual preference, socio-economic background or lifestyle choices. Without empathy, there is discrimination, group hatred, conflict, violence and war. War consumes energy, money, life—masculine energy devouring itself. The Earth needs a stop to war.

"Feminine energy encompasses gentleness and caring for others and the Earth. It can turn the present situation around through understanding, communication and compassion.

"Men need to leave their egos and fighting ways behind. The Earth is at such a crossroads that such needless waste of energy, money and life can only lead to negative consequences.

"With a return to feminine energy and caring for the planet there is still some hope for better times before Earth's man-made darkest night envelopes her."

"Soothing thoughts," I reflect. "Sometimes we go to a hippy festival and everyone seems caring there. Music, dance, nature and spirituality are central to the event. It would be good if the whole world was like that."

"There are positive signs out there, Mya. You just have to look beyond the doom and gloom."

"Cyberbullying is a big problem too," I change the subject, thinking about too many sad stories on the news.

"Yes," agrees Elin, "and needs to be tackled head on. It is very destructive. Victims and those around them need to take action against this and the victim should seek counselling. Perpetrators need to be stopped, legal action taken if possible and they too need counselling. The internet and mobile phones have made it too easy for bullies."

"I know," I reply. "As for terrorism, that is so scary. Those people don't seem to value life."

"Yes, it's very sad. The extremists are causing great trouble all around the world, and it will be a long time before this evil is stamped out. There are so many factors involved. It is a very complex issue."

"Hmm," I acknowledge.

"If there was greater empathy," says Elin, "and a feminine approach of gentle communication, understanding and compassion, I'm sure things would be different."

"I hope things change. As for environmental destruction, loss of species and habitat, that is very depressing."

"I know," agrees Elin, "but again the feminine approach of nurturing would greatly improve things. Indigenous people around the world know the importance of conservation. They are custodians of nature and we all need to learn from them."

"We better hurry up," I muse.

"True. There are some things we can't personally affect, like terrorism or environmental disasters, but we can try to be good and loving spiritual beings with empathy and radiate out our love and light to the world. Positive energy breeds more positive energy and love and light will illuminate the darkness."

"I hope so. Love and light," I smile, "that's you and me Elin."

"Yes, dear love."

"You are truly light. You are my angel Elin."

"Thank you, sweet girl. There are great things in store for you, Mya. I can feel it in my bones."

"Hard to imagine, but I'm glad you believe in me."

"Oh yes, 100 percent," assures Elin.

We meditate, say farewell and I walk home with Sefton, feeling more positive about the world as it is and the future that awaits us.

Chapter Sixteen

NEW HORIZON

At the high school, the year advisor, Mr. Johnston, meets Mum and I in his office. He is a charming, sincere and very helpful man. "So, you've made up your mind, Mya?" he asks, with a welcoming smile.

"Yes, I think this is the place for me."

"That's great. I think you'll be happy here. Here's the enrolment form for you to fill in Joan. Just give it to the receptionist on the way out." Mum proceeds to fill in the form.

"Now, Mya, have you worked out what subjects you want to do?"

"I have," I reply, "though I'd rather stick with my current subjects, but that isn't possible, so I'm going to do history, geography, agriculture and German."

Mr. Johnston writes down my choices. "We can never keep everyone happy with the subjects available on different lines. Here is a map of the school and here is the Year 9 timetable. I'll highlight your subjects for you, Mya." He does so, and then hands me the paperwork.

Mum completes the form and gives it to the receptionist.

"Would you like another tour of the school, Mya?" queries the year advisor. "I can show you where your classes will be."

"Yes, thank you, Mr. Johnston," I reply, enthusiastically.

The recess bell has just gone and older kids are making their way to lockers, laughing, talking. Outside, people are moving all over the place. I appear a little intimidated and Mr. Johnston picks up on this. "Don't worry, Mya. You'll get used to it."

"I hope so."

"Of course, you will," reassures Mum.

The kind man shows us each of the blocks and my classrooms. Some Year 9 kids playing handball recognise me from primary school. "Hi, Mya," they call out, waving.

"Hi," I return the greeting with a shy smile.

Outside the old, red brick main building with imposing, white pillars, Mr. Johnston farewells us beside some well-tended roses.

"Thank you for all your assistance," says Mum.

"Yes, thank you so much," I add.

"You are very welcome. We'll look forward to seeing you next term, Mya. Just come to my room at say, eight forty-five on the Monday, and I'll take you to Roll-call."

"Okay, I'll see you then."

"You will. Bye for now."

"That all went well," says Mum, as she starts the car. "I think you'll be much happier there."

"I hope so. It couldn't get much worse than how it's been lately."

"I know, but you seem much better," acknowledges Mum. "Those walks and horse rides seem to be doing you a lot of good. You always seem better when you come home."

"Yes, it has been helpful," I reply, smiling, but not letting her in on my secret rendezvous with Elin. For some reason, I feel I have to keep that part of my life a secret. It seems sacred and so important that I don't want it to be hampered with or tarnished in any way.

"How about a banana smoothie and pumpkin scones at Emi's Café?" suggests Mum.

"Can't knock that back."

At the cosy café, we enjoy delicious food and each other's company. We don't get much time alone.

This evening, there is a thunderstorm, so no walking or riding. Hopefully, I'll see Elin tomorrow.

I'm looking forward to this new horizon and feel much more peaceful now. Goodnight.

Chapter Seventeen

THE SPIRITUAL LIFE

This is my last week of school. The dark cloud has lifted and I feel optimistic about my future.

After school, I linger in the locker room, waiting for everyone to leave, so I can pile text books into my bag without being noticed. I'll gradually take my books home through the week. I want to depart quietly—not make a big deal of it, and not attract further bullying. My bag is pretty heavy. Waiting for the bus can be painstaking when you really don't want to be there. "Only three more days," I think to myself.

The forest is fresh and shining after the rain yesterday. I take little Casper for a ride this evening, winding through the mountain ash. Ferns are bejeweled with water droplets. For some reason, it is more beautiful and vibrant than ever. Sefton scampers here and there. Elin is sitting on the rock in quiet meditation. I dismount and tie Casper to the poor little wattle tree. He takes a mouthful straight away.

I carefully approach Elin, trying to make as little noise as possible, but a few twigs crunch. She smiles with eyes closed, and then opens them, her eyes are smiling too. "Meditation is useful to attain stillness and oneness with God—to be free of the babble of the mind and rest in that infinite stillness."

"Mm," I nod.

"Meditation may be achieved through peaceful relaxation in nature, gentle exercise, nowness, classes, courses, or listening to guided meditation.

"Your whole life can be a meditative experience as you keep in mind that you are a spiritual being here to learn and give with awareness of your thoughts and feelings and your impact upon other human beings, animals, plants and the Earth.

"Conscious moment-to-moment living with awareness is soulful. A soulful life connects you to God and all that is."

"Yes, and that is so important to me. You, my family, Grace, the horses, Sefton, Whispit, and my spiritual beliefs, have helped pull me through this difficult time lately."

"That's very fortunate. It could have been a lot worse, if not for those relationships and your beliefs."

"I know."

Elin climbs down from the rock and walks, or should I say, glides, over to Casper. She pats his neck and then gives him a little scratch under the chin. He looks like he is meditating now. "Casper likes that," I observe.

"He's a sweet little boy. This evening, I thought I'd focus on the spiritual life, Mya, but first, how did you go at the high school yesterday?"

"It was great, thank you. The Year 9 advisor was very helpful. I'm enrolled now, and I've made my subject choices. The advisor showed me the classrooms I'll be going to, so everything is finalised. It's huge and it seems daunting, but I'm optimistic."

"That's excellent, Mya. So, are you happy to concentrate on the spiritual life this evening?"

"Yes, I'm eager to learn." I sit on a small boulder beside the stream's edge.

Elin sits on a similar rock, close to mine. "Well, to start with, I feel that a life without God may be meaningful to a human being, but a life with

God is enriched and directed. Such a human being becomes fulfilled, at peace and cultivates the nourishment of her soul.

"The spiritual life encompasses dedication and faith in God. It embodies a loving human who cares for others, animals and nature. He finds his talents and shares them with the world to make it a better place. He does the best he can in whatever circumstances he finds himself in while considering the needs and desires of those around him."

I listen intently, and then reflect, "As you said the other day, if people were able to connect more to their spiritual side and live a more soulful life, there wouldn't be so many problems in the world."

"Exactly, dear Mya. Many people don't think beyond their day-to-day existence, and many are driven by their desire for material possessions and status. Others, are not able to see beyond their limited belief structures. Some people have limited spiritual beliefs too, which do not allow them to develop empathy. When people focus on their spirituality, develop greater empathy and a more expansive world view, things may improve for them in their own lives and for those around them. As people become more fulfilled, less things can harm them. It may seem strange, but there is a place for darkness, as contrasts in life are necessary. Without seeing the darkness there would be no appreciation of the light. Lifting the darkness from your soul may propel you towards the light within you and surrounding all that is."

"I see."

Elin stands, and walks away from the rock, gazing into the water. "To care for the soul requires oneness with God, meditation, prayer, simplicity, appreciation and love of self, others, animals, all of nature and God."

I nod in affirmation.

"Prayer connects you to God through speaking to him as your ally in life. Thankfulness, forgiveness, caring for others, the world in general, other countries, nature, assistance—all these things and more can be part of your prayer talk. Don't be afraid. Speak to Him as your dearest friend. He is there for you, always. Prayer enriches the spiritual life."

"I find it helpful," I reflect. "I have always prayed. I try to get Ben to do it before bed. He was happy to when he was younger, but now he's rebelling."

"He may change as he grows older," says Elin. "He has to find his own way through life."

"I know," I reply. "I just wanted to give him a bit of assistance."

"You do that anyway, Mya, just by being you."

"I guess so," I respond, but not convinced.

Elin runs her fingers along a freshly, unfurled fern frond. "Spiritual growth is like the growth of a plant, requiring nurturing, and slowly, little by little, it reaches upward towards the light. Sometimes it may need pruning as it heads in the wrong direction, sometimes growth may stall, but eventually it reaches its magnificence, becoming what it was meant to be, a glowing light upon this Earth, illuminating all that it comes into contact with, walking beside God, in godliness."

"As you are Elin."

"Maybe," she smiles, looking shyly at the pebbles below her feet. Always humble, this amazing angel friend of mine. I feel very blessed to have met her and to have experienced all this wisdom.

"Beautiful words," I add.

"Thank you, Mya. Here is a little poem for you." Elin hands me a neatly folded piece of paper.

I open it and read aloud,

"God is there

Upon the dew on a spider's web on a winter morning

In the gurgling water falling over boulders

In a stranger's smile

> With the autumn falling leaves and the winter crackling fire
>
> As the sun sets and twilight glows
>
> God is there, an all loving, all-encompassing God."

"That is lovely," I acknowledge.

"Just a little poem to reassure you when things get difficult. Here is another one in the same vein." Elin hands me another neatly folded piece of paper, grainy recycled paper.

I read,

> "I see God
>
> I see God in the smiling eyes of a child in the Nepalese mountains
>
> I see God in the complexity of the rainforest in Malaysia
>
> I see God in city streets
>
> I feel Him as I walk
>
> He is there, with us all, all the time
>
> He just needs to hear your call, to open your eyes to him. Feel that love
>
> In faith is love and oneness."

"That's also beautiful. Thank you, Elin." I stand up and give her a little hug.

"You're welcome, sweet girl."

"I've talked to you about nowness previously," says Elin, as she resumes her position sitting on the boulder. "I believe it is an important part of living a spiritual life. Nowness is living with full awareness in present time with attention to others and the environment around you. Listening attentively is cultivating, as is empathy.

"Focusing on tasks without distraction in nowness helps you live the spiritual life, as does doing things you love, following your chosen life path with passion, and taking time to be joy-filled and giving by undertaking things such as visiting an elderly relative, making a cake with your children, writing a card to a distant friend, volunteering, or greeting a lonely old man. This is spiritual work as much as meditation and prayer. We are in the human body to experience this physical world and our inter-connectedness enriches our soulful life.

"Doing what you love, whether for work or pleasure, connects you to the spiritual as your soul draws sustenance and you are in nowness as you paint, ski, gallop your horse, play with your children, walk, build a house, create a garden, or communicate with a customer. There are many ways to nourish your soul, but make it a priority, and you will attain greater harmony, peace and wellbeing.

"Create moments of peace and stillness—yes, stillness. This will nourish your soul. As will a simple life. Complications and too many possessions crowd your time and thoughts. Simplify, and your life will nurture your soul.

"A soulful life connects you to God and all that is."

I nod in agreement, trying to absorb all this information and trying to remember as much of it as possible to write in my journal. "That's a lot to take in Elin, but I'll try to remember all that inspirational knowledge."

"Don't worry too much, Mya. I have a little handbook which I will give you one day soon. It has little reminders of everything we have talked about over these past weeks."

"That will be very helpful. It's been a lot for a 14-year-old to take in."

"I know that, but I also know you are capable of absorbing and understanding it. Your sensitivity and openness stand you in good stead."

Now it's my turn to be humble and I smile shyly, "Thank you, Elin."

"There is just one more topic I want to cover before we say good evening—death."

"Death?" I query, looking somewhat aghast.

"Well, it's an important topic, and too often pushed under the carpet, especially in modern, western society, but it needs to be thought about, possibly meditated upon, discussed and one's own death, contemplated."

"That's something I don't like to think about too much. I've had to deal with it, losing animals and elderly relatives, but it's something that seems so far away that I put it out of my mind. I'm afraid of death. It all seems so scary and unknown," I reveal my private fear.

"Death is not to be feared," reassures Elin. "It is a doorway to a new beginning and onward growth of the soul.

"Contemplation of death leads to an appreciation of life. If you know death is near, or contemplate its approach, the layers of your life may peel away down to the bare essentials of what makes you happy, what is important and what gives you peace.

"Life involves the gradual letting go—letting go of youth, material possessions, old ideas, outworn relationships, physical and mental capacities, outgrown lifestyles and loved ones. Letting go can be difficult and emotional but at the same time liberating as life becomes simpler, allowing greater time for soulful pursuits.

"The ultimate release is the release of the body at death. Do not be afraid."

I'm quiet for a moment and then say, "That's reassuring, but it's still scary to think about leaving everything familiar behind and entering into another unknown existence."

"Of course," replies Elin. "I'm sure most people feel that way at some time, but you will be supported, and there will be guidance all the way. That's a whole different topic, and not a short one."

"Mm," I agree.

Light is fading rapidly. The days are shortening now. "You better get going soon, Mya."

I walk over to Casper and untie him from the now extra ragged wattle.

"I'm going away for two weeks to a spiritual conference at a beautiful resort near the ocean in Queensland," says Elin. "I'm looking forward to the warmth and tropical atmosphere."

"That sounds great," I reply.

"I'm leaving tomorrow, and will be back in a couple of weeks. You'll be on holidays then, won't you, Mya?"

"Yes, thank goodness."

Elin smiles. "Are you going away anywhere?"

"I'm going to visit my grandfather on his farm for a few days. That's all. He has a lovely, old, black stock horse that I ride. It's a nice change from home. I help my grandfather with cattle work and I enjoy spending time with him. He's a very knowledgeable man."

"That sounds good, Mya. Well, I'll see you in a couple of weeks then."

"You will. Thank you, Elin."

My wise teacher gives me a quick squeeze. I mount up and wave goodbye as I trot off into the cool evening with Sefton running by Casper's side.

It's completely dark when I enter the kitchen. "You're very late today," observes Mum gruffly, as she stirs a bolognaise sauce. "You shouldn't stay out so late, Mya. We'll worry about you and have to send out a search party."

"I'm sorry, Mum. The days just aren't long enough."

"At least you have holidays soon, so you can do lots of riding and walking then," her voice softens a little.

"Yeah, and I'm looking forward to going to Grandfather's place as well."

"We'll call him tonight, so we can work out the final plans," says Mum. Pausing, she adds, "What is it about these late rides and walks, Mya? You don't normally do that so often."

"It's just helped me a lot while I've been having a hard time at school," I explain, as I go to the fridge to get out salad vegetables. "The forest and the stream soothe my heart and mind. I escape from my problems and feel happier there."

"Alright, I understand, but next term we'll have to put an end to that. Winter is coming and it'll just be getting too dark."

"Okay, Mum." Maybe I'll only be able to see Elin on weekends then.

Tonight, I have a job remembering today's teachings about living the spiritual life. I write down as much as possible. That handbook would be "handy". Exhausted, I hit the pillow, falling asleep almost immediately.

Chapter Eighteen

LAST DAYS

I just live through the last days, generally looking forward to it being over, but I will miss Grace, some of the boys and a few of the teachers.

I continue to pile my books into my bag after school. On Wednesday, it looks particularly heavy. The nastiest girl from the group had previously been a student at the high school. "Are you leaving, Mya? Too hard for you here is it? Are you going to the high school next term?" I think she had heard it on the grapevine.

"Hmm," I give a little nod, and whisper my reply, heaving my bag across the playground.

"We're just too good for you here aren't we?" she continues.

Again, I nod, and walk quickly to the gate. I'm glad Mum is picking me up. My eyes are glistening with tears.

As I open the car door, Mum sees my look of anguish. "Oh Mya. Have those girls caused you trouble again?"

"Just the nastiest one," I mumble, as I get in. "She knows I'm leaving, and she was making a big deal of it."

"Don't worry. Two days to go and it'll all be over," reassures Mum. "Actually, you can skip Friday if you like. They know you're leaving now. You don't even have to go tomorrow if you don't want to."

"No, I want to go. I haven't said all my goodbyes yet. There's a few people I want to talk to."

"Alright, Mya. Let's go to Emi's. That chocolate caramel slice looks extra delicious right now."

"Okay Mum, thanks."

Thursday is not so bad. I meet up with Grace at recess and thank her for all her support and interest in me. She gives me a little hug and hopes we'll keep in touch. Like Elin, she reminds me of an angel. I'll miss her heaps. She's so gentle and kind, different to so many of the other girls.

At lunchtime, I tell my handball buddies of my departure. They're surprised. They all know kids at the high school and they say they are happy there. One boy seems particularly disappointed—I think he likes me.

Telling my three favourite teachers is even harder. The old history teacher is very sympathetic. "You've had a hard time here, Mya. It's understandable that you're leaving. I wish you well in whatever you hope to achieve. You're a good girl. You deserve better things."

"Thank you for all your help," I reply. "I'll miss your class."

"I'll miss you too."

The elderly, Dutch agriculture teacher is also surprised, but he wishes me well. He is a character.

The art teacher is very sorry I'm leaving. He's been nurturing my possible talent. "Keep doing your artwork won't you?"

"I'm not doing it as a subject, but I'll try to keep doing it at home and maybe do a TAFE course."

"I hope so. If you have a talent it is important to nurture it and allow your creativity to flow." He sounds like Elin. Have they had contact???

"I know. I'll try to do that. The choice was agriculture or art unfortunately. I chose ag as it's not so easy to study it outside of school."

"True, but please, Mya, don't allow your talent to become latent."

"I'll try not to. Thank you for all your help. I've really enjoyed your classes."

"You are welcome. We'll miss you over here and your potential artwork."

I say goodbye and walk away from the spacious art rooms, feeling a sense of loss about this part of my life being over, for now.

I'm glad it's the last time I'll have to wait for the bus, watching the clock hand slowly crawling. Come on 4 p.m. On the bus, I look out the window for the last time at the cream buildings, manicured gardens and green ovals. I will miss the pleasant atmosphere but not some of the things that go on within it. I look ahead, looking forward to change and a brighter, happier future.

Chapter Nineteen

HOLIDAYS

Now that I've left that school, a huge weight is off my shoulders. I'm a bit nervous about starting at the high school, but I have two weeks of holidays before that.

We drive up to Grandfather's farm, which is about an hour away from home, high in the hills and very remote. I love going there. It's a world away from our farm and our town. We wind along the quiet road beside the river overlooking a lush valley with steep hills rising above. Some are blanketed with forest. Others are open paddocks with black Angus and Murray Grey cattle grazing—black and grey dots in the distance.

We reach the dirt road leading to Grandfather's farm—only five kilometres to go. Ben and I are really excited now.

Grandfather is waiting for us at the bottom of his neat garden. He waves a welcoming greeting, as he holds his fox terrier, Rhonda, in his arms. Grandfather is a tall and fit man with dark hair and a moustache, a retired army colonel, who is quite strict. He is a proud man who is very knowledgeable, and he has led a full life, retiring to this farm a few years ago. Dad, being a hippy, didn't go down too well.

As we get out of the car, Grandfather puts Rhonda down. She barks excitedly, running around and wagging her tail effervescently in terrier style. "Settle down Rhonda," admonishes Grandfather. We exchange hugs. "It's good to see you all. I'm getting a bit of cabin fever."

"Well, now you've got Mya to keep you company for a while," says Mum.

"Yes, I've been looking forward to that. How long are you staying, Mya?"

"Maybe a week," I shrug.

"Great. I'll drive you home next weekend if you like."

"Thanks, Grandfather."

"I need to pick up supplies, and remind myself that society is still out there."

"I would go stir crazy living up here," says Dad.

"That doesn't happen to me," replies Grandfather. "I've got lots to keep me busy, and books to read, but I miss intellectual conversation at times."

"You can educate Mya this week," suggests Mum.

I frown.

"We'll see about that," chuckles Grandfather. He picks up my bag and carries it up the steps onto the old verandah which adjoins my room. Inside, he places it beside an antique, oak cupboard. There is a blue patchwork quilt on the bed and the view out to the hills through the small window is glorious. I love it here.

The house is an old, white weatherboard, very homely and old fashioned. It's set in a small valley surrounded by steep, grazing country and forest beyond.

"I've got lamb in the oven. It's time for lunch," says Grandfather, ushering us through the sitting-room into the kitchen where the table is set and the delicious aroma of hot roast beckons. Grandfather always puts in 100 percent effort with everything he does. He gets the lamb out of the oven for Dad to carve and proceeds to make gravy. A homemade apple pie is sitting on the bench. My mouth waters in anticipation of this delicious feast. Ben goes to grab a crunchy potato. "No, you don't boy," scolds Grandfather.

"Sorry," apologises Ben, looking downwards.

"You should know better," observes Grandfather.

"He does," says Mum. "Those potatoes look just too irresistible, don't they Ben?"

My brother nods in agreement.

Dad changes the subject. "Cattle prices are good at the moment."

"Yes," agrees Grandfather. "I'm selling steers in a few weeks, so I hope they stay that way."

"We've had good autumn rain, so prices should remain high," reflects Dad.

We all sit at the table and Grandfather serves lunch. He joins us, says grace, and then we dive in, enjoying our delectable meal.

"Joan said you're changing schools, Mya," says Grandfather.

"Yes, I start at the high school next term."

"That's a shame. I thought that school was very good for you."

"In some ways it was, but I didn't really have any friends there in the end." Mum and I fill Grandfather in on the events of the past term.

"Sometimes, you just have to tough it out," observes Grandfather. "Things have to change eventually."

"I know, but I'm just not that strong and, as you all say, I'm too sensitive."

"Well, I hope things are better next term."

"Thank you, Grandfather. I hope so too."

We talk about farming, aunts, uncles and cousins spread all over Australia, the result of army life, and terrible things happening in the world right now.

After the main course, Mum gets up to clear the table. "No, no, Joan. I'll do it," says Grandfather, the ever-proud host.

Soon, he is back with the steaming apple pie, ice cream and lashings of rich, fresh, local cream. You can't buy it in the supermarkets like that. Ben and I love the hot pie with cold ice cream and cream, eating silently, savouring every mouthful of that delicious contrast. Mm. Afterwards, we are like content, sleepy, purring cats lazing in the sun.

Later, we go for a drive up the steep hills in the old four-wheel-drive Toyota ute. Blackberries and ferns are a bit of a problem. Grandfather has a herd of goats to try to keep them under control. Ben and I ride in the back, enjoying the fresh air. The views are beautiful with the valley below and the odd farm house dotted here and there. It gets so steep it's scary, as we climb the rough, stony track. We hold on tightly.

At the top of the hill, we stop, get out and walk a little. A wedge-tailed eagle is wheeling on a thermal. I admire its magnificence. The amazing bird begins to drop in altitude. Suddenly, the eagle is only two metres above my head, its talons frighteningly close, wings outstretched for three metres, as it hovers, looking at me intently. It's awe-inspiring, but is way too close for comfort. "Go away, go away," I beg, adding a scream, as I crouch down trying to escape.

Grandfather picks up a stick, and waves it at the imposing bird of prey. "Off you go, eagle," he urges.

The eagle eyes him for a moment, and then flies off towards a dead gum tree.

"Phew, I'm glad that's over," I sigh with relief. "That was scary."

"I've never seen anything like that before," observes Grandfather. "I guess he was curious."

"Way too curious," I add.

"Well, you'll never forget that will you, Mya?" says Dad.

"No, I won't." My heart is still racing as we climb back into the ute.

We drive into the forest, enjoying the fresh, eucalyptus filled, mountain air. I breathe it in deeply. I love this place so much.

Back at the house, we enjoy Grandfather's rock cakes for afternoon tea, though they are a bit teeth unfriendly, and could be re-named cement cakes.

Ben and I go to see the house goats, who have frames around their necks to stop them getting into the garden. Grandfather said the electric fence was turned off. I go to pat a nanny through the fence. Zap. I'm knocked to the ground, screaming with the jolt of pain. Ben holds his belly laughing, almost joining me. "It's not funny, Ben. That really hurt." He continues to giggle. Little brothers, I don't know.

Soon, it's time for my family to drive home. We hug goodbye. Grandfather and I wave as they head down the little valley until they're out of sight. "How's Zulu?" I ask him.

"He's fine, and eagerly waiting for his rider." Zulu is a solid, black, aged Australian Stock Horse. Grandfather gave him that name, which I thought was a bit racist, but it suits the proud gelding. "Let's go and see him."

"Okay," I readily agree.

Zulu is in the paddock beyond the old stables. Ancient peppercorn trees imbue the air with their peppery fragrance. "Hello, Zulu." I give the shiny, black horse a hug, my arms wrapped around his thick neck.

"You can ride tomorrow morning if you like," suggests Grandfather.

"That sounds good," I reply.

I saddle up Zulu and ride down the dirt road. He's a lovely, quiet horse but not lazy. It's nice to be riding somewhere different. He has a rocking horse canter and I enjoy a long lope through the pretty countryside.

The days pass quickly. I help Grandfather move the cattle, me on Zulu, him in the old ute. One day, we drive up through the forest, back to eagle territory. Another day, we visit a small town where Grandfather has to meet up with his livestock agent. At night, we discuss literature, world events and foreign countries. Grandfather has much to tell, and I enjoy this one-on-one time with him.

Too soon, it's time to head home. Grandfather drives me back to our farm, where Mum greets us, "I hope Mya behaved herself."

"Of course, she did," replies Grandfather. "She's a very self-contained girl. She likes to ride, walk and read, so never gets bored like so many other kids would up there."

"Yes," agrees Mum. "Many couldn't handle being away from computers and mobile phones."

We enjoy Mum's chicken Maryland and toffee sponge. Later, we say goodbye at the gate. "Thank you, Grandfather for the best week." I give him a hug.

"You're very welcome. I'll look forward to you coming next holidays, and hopefully with some good news about your new school."

"Should be good news."

Grandfather heads into town. Part of me still wants to be up in that valley, riding Zulu, enjoying the fresh air in the forest, my cosy room, and special conversation. I still have a week to go at home. I should make the most of it.

On Friday, I meet up with Elin who is sitting on the rock beside the stream. She is looking more radiant than ever. "Hello, Mya."

"Hi, Elin. You are looking well."

"Nothing like a bit of Queensland warmth and sunshine to uplift the soul. The conference was fantastic."

"Did you learn much?"

"Some new ideas but the best part was that there were people there from all over the world with different religious and spiritual traditions, open to sharing ideas and discussing different practices. It was very positive when you compare it to what is happening in the world out there right now, with so much discrimination, violence, wars, terrorism, global warming and environmental destruction. These people all cared deeply for others, the environment and the world in general. It made me feel more optimistic about things."

"That's great, Elin. How did they run the conference?" I ask, as I sit on the rock opposite her.

"Every morning, there was a meditation followed by a prayer meeting. After breakfast there was a lecture, each day given by a teacher of a different tradition, and then a discussion, chanting and another meditation. After lunch there was free time, meditation and prayer time. At night there were discussion groups and a final meditation. It was a great experience."

"It sounds like it."

"The resort was beautiful too. It had lovely tropical gardens with little Buddhist and Hindu statues dotted here and there, and it was overlooking a lovely beach. We could always hear the gentle lapping of waves breaking on the shore. It was on a small inlet, so there wasn't any surf."

"I want to go there," I enthuse.

"They have the conference every year, so you can when you get a bit older."

"I'll look forward to that."

"How was your time at your grandfather's farm?"

"I loved it. I did lots of riding on old Zulu, helped Grandfather with cattle work and enjoyed talking to him about books, history, the current world situation and foreign countries."

"That's great, Mya. Do you remember me talking about respect for the elderly?"

"Vaguely."

"Just a quick reminder. There is lack of respect for the elderly in modern, western culture. Not so in Asia or India, where the elderly are revered and cared for within the family. This needs to be turned around. We need to love, care for and respect the elderly—they are a wealth of knowledge and potential teachers—not just the faceless old to be pushed into retirement villages and nursing homes to await their death."

"I agree," I reply. "There needs to be more care and respect."

"That reminds me," says Elin, as she reaches into her white, cotton shoulder bag. "I've got this little handbook for you, Mya, to help remind you of the many things we've talked about recently." She hands me a small book. On the cover is a white crane standing amongst reeds on an estuary bank with a watery background.

"Thank you, Elin. I'll cherish it." I flick through the pages, reading the chapter headings, and quickly glimpse some wise words. "Sounds like you Elin." No author is mentioned.

"Oh, it's an old book I've learnt things from, and now you can too."

"Thank you," I pause, and then remember something else I wanted to ask Elin about. "There was a strange thing that happened at Grandfather's farm…" I describe the incident with the wedge-tailed eagle. "It was amazing but at the same time pretty scary," I complete the story.

"That's very interesting, and it sounds like a fortunate experience for you, Mya. According to some traditions, eagles represent God. They are the king of the skies. If you have such an encounter, which is extremely rare, the eagle has something to teach you. In your case, it may have been to tell you to fly close to God, defeat your fears and see beyond the horizon. Have faith in your purpose and how all things, good and bad, fit into the picture of your life. The eagle teaches true sight. He says, *Step off the cliff and fly with me. Use my wings. I will take you on the journey within. Trust me, and then you will know the way to wholeness. I am in you as you are in me. We are one. I am one with God.* The eagle is connected with the air element, which symbolises communication and thought. It represents a unique and independent spirit, and it says, to reclaim this strength, you need to shrug off everyday burdens that keep you from flying free. You are blessed to have had this experience, Mya. The eagle has much to teach you."

"Wow, that's amazing. I know animals represent different things, but I didn't know it was to such a great extent."

"Oh yes, and much more, but that's enough for now. Let's do a meditation," suggests Elin.

"Okay," I agree.

We sit silently on the rock, concentrating on our breathing, stillness, the observer beyond the mind, absorbed by nowness and oneness.

The autumn coolness envelops us. We open our eyes. "It's time to go home," says Elin.

"Yep. Mum's not too happy about my late walks and rides. She's threatening to send out a search party."

"We better not let that happen," chuckles Elin. "These meetings are too important."

"Very much so," I agree.

"I'll meet you here next Friday, if the weather is okay, but earlier, around 4:15 p.m.?" suggests Elin.

"Okay. The new bus gets me home earlier, and I'll assign some chores to Ben. Could be hard, but I'll try."

A little hug and goodnight.

I read the handbook under lamplight. It all rings true, and seems so Elin. She is still a bit of a mystery, a very wise mystery. Goodnight.

Chapter Twenty

CHANGE

I'm all ready for school—new uniform, new bag, new books. I feel apprehensive but also optimistic. Dad drives me there in his expensive, new Volvo. I get him to drop me off a block away—don't want to be seen getting out of that. Don't want to attract unwanted attention and provide fuel for bullies.

Out the front of the school, seniors are mingling, happily greeting each other after the break. Other kids head to different parts of the playground. I walk up the steps of the imposing, main building. It's daunting. At Mr. Johnston's office, his friendly smile and familiarity calms me a little. "Hello, Mya. Are you ready for the new term?"

"As ready as I'll ever be," I reply, shyly.

"How were your holidays?" asks the Year 9 advisor.

"Great, thank you. I visited my grandfather on his farm. And yours?"

"I had an enjoyable time. My family and I went to Thailand. It was my kids first time to go overseas, so it was an eye-opener for them, but they loved it."

I nod and smile.

"I'll take you to your Roll-call class and introduce you to your teacher and the students."

"Okay, thank you." Trepidation.

The bell rings and the corridors are soon full of kids going to lockers and their Roll-call classes. So many more kids at this school.

At my Roll-call class, Mr. Johnston introduces me to my lovely, young teacher, and to the whole class. A couple of girls smile in recognition, remembering me from primary school. One beckons me over to sit beside her, a sweet girl named Belinda. The teacher calls the roll, and then tells us of events coming up over the term.

When the bell rings, Belinda asks what subjects I'm doing. I tell her, and coincidentally, she is doing the same, except for German. We're also in the same English and Maths class, so that is very helpful. "We've got English first," says Belinda. "Follow me." I tag along with her small group of friends who all seem to be very friendly and down-to-earth.

Everything is more casual here—don't have to stand up when the teachers enter the room and wait to be told when to sit down. It all seems a bit weird and foreign to me. Will take a while to get used to it.

At recess we sit in a courtyard where I recognise another girl from near home who I've occasionally met out horse riding. She is very nice too, and her friends are horse riders. I feel optimistic about new friendships.

Belinda keeps an eye on me and helps me find my way around the school. She's a very caring girl.

My new bus is at the school at 3:30 p.m. We pick up kids at a few other schools, and then head out to our rural area.

At teatime, Mum and Dad are keen to hear about my day. "It was a bit daunting at first. It's a huge school, and there are so many kids there. Mr. Johnston was very welcoming. He took me to my Roll-call class and introduced me to the teacher and kids there. Belinda from primary school was in that class, and she's in most of my classes, so she took me under her wing and made sure I was in the right place at the right time. She is really nice and so are her friends. There are a few girls from farms there too, and they like horse riding."

"That sounds very good, Mya. And what about the teachers?" asks Mum.

"They were generally quite young, enthusiastic and not so strict though the geography teacher runs his class like the army. He has short, brown hair, a moustache and is very neatly dressed. I was told he also runs cadets."

"You need someone to keep them in line," laughs Dad.

"There are a few boys in that class who are a challenge for him."

The week rolls on smoothly. I am re-establishing old friendships and making new ones. Soon I have ten good friends. The German class is a bit of a disappointment. One girl is fluent in German, a few of us want to learn, and I think the other girls are just there because they thought they could bludge, so ruin it for everyone by mucking up all the time. The teacher is a middle-aged, short, thin, quiet and gentle German man who seems to be overwhelmed by their behaviour. I'm worried he may have a nervous breakdown. There is no way the kids would get away with this at the other school.

Other differences are no choir, no musicals or plays, and no pressure to play sport. I miss the cultural aspect. If kids don't do their homework, repercussions are few. The atmosphere is different too. The buildings are not so inviting—more like a concrete jungle.

The geography teacher is definitely tested by those boys. One cheeky, blonde-haired boy, who reminds me a lot of Ben, talks back to him all the time and makes jokes which have the whole class laughing. One day, the teacher yells at him and gets him to stand outside with his nose on a specific brick. The boy isn't tall and puts his nose on a lower brick. The teacher yells, "No, that brick." The boy almost has to stand on tippy toes to reach the brick. Still not good enough. "That brick," roars the colonel, pointing at one even higher. The boy manages, just. The teacher returns to the class, red-faced, and we have to fight to contain our laughter. Stony silence ensues as we read the text book.

I'm envious of the kids doing art, but I'm enjoying agriculture, and especially love going over to the school farm. We have a lovely female teacher and it's a small class.

You can't have everything it seems, and to be happy is more important than anything else at my age.

On Friday, I coerce Ben into quickly helping me do the chores. He moans and groans but helps me get them done at super speed.

I walk quickly down the narrow path with Sefton scampering here and there. It's a cool evening. The days are getting really short now. Elin is at our special place, sitting on the rock. She's wearing a warm grey jumper and corduroys. "Hello, Mya."

"Hi, Elin."

"How has your week been?" asks Elin.

"It's been challenging but positive," I reply, as I join Elin on the rock. "I've met up with old friends from primary school and made new ones. The teachers have been really nice and helpful. Such a different and large school takes a bit of getting used to, but I'm adjusting. I miss the cultural things and my art classes. It's not so strict either. I'm not sure if that's a good or bad thing."

"Well, overall it sounds positive," says Elin. "I think you will be much happier there."

"So far, so good."

"Excellent."

"How was your week Elin?"

"It's been busy. I've been working in my garden and doing some writing."

"Oh, what are you writing about?"

"Just some reflections after being at the spiritual conference. It consolidated some of my ideas and put a different perspective on others."

"Sounds interesting. I'd like to read it."

"You can, when it's completed," says Elin.

"I'll look forward to that."

We talk about my animals, the weather, just simple things. That brings to mind one of my favourite Elin quotes, *To care for the soul requires oneness with God, meditation, prayer, simplicity, appreciation and love of self, others, animals, all of nature and God.*

I remember something else. "After talking about the eagle last week, that made me think of another question."

"What's that, Mya?"

"Another animal, well insect, that pops into my life frequently is the ladybird. They often land on me, and sometimes in the strangest places, like the middle of the city. Ben and I used to collect them from a Japanese maple tree in our garden. It was so green and we enjoyed climbing it and catching the little beetles, and then kept them in jars with leaves and water droplets, trying to keep them as pets, but they didn't survive. They're funny creatures. They used to play dead. I think I've created some bad karma there."

"Oh Mya, you were young and innocent," laughs Elin. "Don't worry. Leaves wouldn't have done it for the ladybird. They need insects, like aphids. Farmers love them because they are great pest devourers."

"Oh, I didn't know that," I reply. "Anyway, I was wondering, does the ladybird have any particular significance as I find it a bit strange how they always appear in my life?"

"You are fortunate," observes Elin. "The ladybird is also often referred to as the ladybeetle, which was given its name in the Middle Ages—the beetle of our lady. It was dedicated to the Virgin Mary. The ladybeetle has a link to spiritual ideals and religious devotion. Prayer and meditation are recommended. It has a short life cycle of only one month and it teaches us to release worries and enjoy life to the fullest. It is a messenger of promise, to reconnect us to the joy of living, and tells us to allow God to enter our lives. The ladybeetle brings luck and abundance. The Universe is conspiring in serendipitous ways."

"Maybe like our meeting one another," I suggest.

"Yes, that's an example," agrees Elin. "The ladybeetle also represents the child-like nature in everyone. You can delight in small things and be happy by yourself."

"Well, that part is true."

"You can spread your wings and bring blessings and hope to others," continues Elin. "There is magic in the Universe. The power of believing is your magic, and you will realise that inner happiness is the most rewarding of all things. The ladybeetle is a symbol of taking action on your dreams. It is a beautiful energy to be connected to, Mya, and it will add to your blessings in life I'm sure."

"There's a lot to it, but it all sounds positive," I smile.

Climbing down from the rock, I observe, "There'll be trouble at home if I don't get going."

My mentor follows me. "Yes, we better only meet on the weekends from now on," she suggests.

"Hm, it's too dark too soon now," I agree.

"How about Sunday week, around 2 p.m.?"

"Sounds good. I'll probably ride one of the horses."

We hug and farewell one another.

I walk swiftly home with Sefton.

Mum is setting the table as I enter the kitchen. She scowls, "What did I tell you, Mya?"

"I know Mum. I'm sorry. That'll be the last time, I promise."

"It better be, or there'll be no more of it at all."

Over tea, I tell my family of the boy with the brick incident. They nearly fall off their chairs laughing.

I'm sleeping much better now—not so worried. Goodnight.

Chapter Twenty-one

LOOKING FORWARD

Six months later

I meet Elin the following Sunday and most Sundays for the rest of the year. She continues to support me and we revisit many of the ideas she had talked about previously. It would have been difficult to get through the year without her.

School is good. I'm happy there. I have lots of friends and I drift a bit between groups, but that doesn't seem to worry anyone. I'm doing a little art course at TAFE, which satisfies that urge somewhat. I have a new horse riding friend which is fantastic. My life is much better now. I get a bit lazy with my school work. I need to work on that one.

On a Sunday in November, I tie Casper to the wattle tree. Sefton does his usual exploring. Elin is in her white dress and looks lovely. She greets me with a hug and seems a lot more serious than usual. "There's something I have to tell you, Mya."

"What is it?" I ask, feeling apprehensive.

"I'm sorry, Mya," Elin apologises. I have no idea what she is leading up to.

"Please Elin, just tell me. It's okay."

"I have to return to my home country," she replies, quietly. "My father is unwell, and I need to help my mother."

"Is it a permanent thing?" I become teary.

"I'm afraid so, Mya. I didn't really know how long I would be in Australia. I love it here, but I'm needed at home. I miss the pine forest, the deer, the autumn leaves, wild herbs and my very dear and now very old spiritual teacher. There is a time for all things, and this time has come."

The tears are flowing down my cheeks now. "Will I ever see you again?" I manage to splutter.

Elin's eyes are misty too. "Of course. I'll come back one day, and you can visit me when you're older. We can keep in touch on Skype. I'm a natural woman, but I can cope a little with technology."

"Well, at least we won't lose contact," I manage a little smile.

"No, definitely not."

I try to compose myself. "When are you leaving Elin?"

"Next weekend. It's all very sudden, but my father doesn't have much time left, and I want to be there for my parents. I'm satisfied with the time I've had here."

"I've benefited greatly. I think I'm the luckiest girl around this area."

"Oh, you're too sweet," says Elin, hugging me. "Shall we sit down for a while?"

"Okay," I agree. We climb onto the rock and settle into our usual spots.

"As this is one of our last meetings, I would like to talk a little about the future."

"Please do. Go on," I urge.

"As we look at the world as it is, the outlook may seem dismal with so many wars, terrorism, discrimination, persecution, poverty, inequality, environmental destruction, species extinction and being threatened with extinction, global warming, pollution, rampant materialism, alienating urban life for many and social problems abounding.

"There is hope if we can all become more soulful, tune into our spirituality and feel empathy for all of humanity, animals and nature. With that so many problems would diminish.

"A feminine energy needs to embrace planet Earth so that no longer the aggressive, dominating and materialistic male energy wreaks havoc.

With the feminine energy will come a caring attitude to all of life and a harmonious existence may ensue—but time is of the essence—the time is now."

"I hope that happens," I respond. "When you watch the news, it's hard to imagine that anything is going to change."

"I know," agrees Elin, "but if everyone had that attitude there would be no hope. There are many individuals and groups working towards change, and eventually, the light has to overcome the prevailing darkness."

"I hope so."

"Faith is important, Mya. Faith in yourself, those you are close to, and above all, faith in God."

"Mm."

"Shall we do a quick meditation?"

"Okay." We lose ourselves in oneness, us in God and God in us, Mya and Elin, reaching towards the light.

Climbing down from the rock, Elin says, "I will see you on Wednesday and next Saturday, if that suits, Mya?"

"Definitely. I wouldn't miss it for the world. You have meant so much to me, Elin. I'll miss you, but knowing I'll see you in the future, and that we can Skype, means it doesn't seem so bad." I climb down too.

"I know," says Elin, giving me a farewell hug. She unties Casper's reins and hands them to me. I mount up, call Sefton, urge the pony into a canter and disappear into the forest with tears streaming down my cheeks.

As she serves tea, Mum senses there's something wrong. "What's up, Mya?"

"Oh, just a bit too much self-reflection. I still have the odd bad day, but I'll be alright tomorrow."

"Are you sure?" queries Mum.

"Yes, I'm sure," I smile in response.

Saturday is our final meeting. I tie Goldie up and greet Elin. "Are you all ready for your trip home?"

"Yes, everything is organised. I just have to say goodbye to my neighbours. I have something for you, Mya." Elin reaches into her shoulder bag. "Here you are." She hands me a small, neatly wrapped parcel in white cloth tied with hemp.

I hold the gift for a moment. "Unwrap it," urges Elin.

I do so, slowly, to reveal a gleaming, white crystal. Light exudes from it and it has a magical quality. I am surprised and almost drop the glimmering stone.

"Careful," says Elin. "That is one of my wisdom stones. It will lead you to knowledge and magic, Mya. It will help you connect to God and all that is. When you feel sad or confused, pick up the stone and meditate. It will help give you peace and guidance, at the same time connecting us."

I'm in awe, looking at this glistening, precious object. "Thank you, Elin. It's perfect, and so special. I'll cherish it."

"You are welcome, Mya. Let's do a quick meditation with the stone."

We sit on the earth beside the rock amongst ferns with the gurgling white water singing its watery song. Eucalyptus fills the fresh air. We focus on the stone, and soon are absorbed by overwhelming white light, filling us with peace and a sense of belonging. It's blissful.

Re-emerging from our bliss, we smile knowing smiles. Distance and time will not part us. We stand and talk about everyday things.

"Thank you, Elin, for being a shining light in my life this year. You are amazing."

"No, you are amazing, dear love," she replies, pointing at me.

I smile. "I have a little gift for you too." I walk over to the saddle-bag and take out the flat gift, wrapped in silver paper and tied with red ribbon. Elin is leaning on the granite rock. The sun pierces through the silver-rimmed clouds and all of a sudden, everything is very silvery, the quartz gleaming out from the sparkling granite. I hand the gift to Elin.

She unwraps it carefully. "Oh, it's beautiful," she says, holding a small painting of us sitting on the rock beside the stream with Goldie tied up to a wattle and Sefton sitting nearby. "Did you do this, Mya?"

"Yes," I reply, shyly.

"It's very good."

"Thank you. I just wanted to give you a little reminder of our time together."

"It's perfect. I'll hang it in my bedroom. Thank you, Mya. That will be on the plane with me. Taking no risks with that one."

I nod and smile.

"I have to go, Mya. I'm sorry, but you know how it is when you have a big journey ahead."

"Yes, and moving as well," I acknowledge.

"I'll Skype you next Saturday at 3 p.m. your time, is that okay?" asks Elin.

"That'll be great," I reply. "Thank you, Elin, for being my teacher and support in so many ways."

"You've been an excellent student, very open, and keen to learn. I've got a lot out of it too, you know, Mya. Believe in yourself, your dreams, God's love and magic. Life will be good to you, Mya. I'm sure of it, as are the eagle and the ladybeetle. Your future will shine."

I'm overwhelmed and teary as I walk over to Goldie and pat her neck. She nuzzles up to me, sensing my sadness.

"You better go," urges Elin, gently. This was never going to be easy.

A final hug, and I look into those oceanic, blue eyes, for the last time, for now.

I mount up. "Thank you. Have a safe journey. Bye Elin."

"Good luck, Mya. Goodbye, sweet girl."

I push Goldie into a trot. The golden dog obediently follows for a change. He must sense the situation. I turn back for a final wave. My glorious teacher returns it.

Tears. I'm an emotional creature. I'm okay—it's just that I'm going to miss her so much.

Over the following weeks, then months, we Skype. Elin helps her parents, and goes on to set up an alternative school. She continues her spiritual work and I continue working towards my dream of becoming a writer and an artist.

 With love, Mya and Elin.

www.ingramcontent.com/pod-product-compliance
Lightning Source LLC
Chambersburg PA
CBHW050313010526
44107CB00055B/2219